WEEKDAY GOURMET

MEALS IN MINUTES

THE WEEKDAY GOURMET

Lawry's understands that today's lifestyles are busy. That's why we designed the Weekday Gourmet—for people on the go who still love to sit down to a home-cooked meal. With Lawry's WEEKDAY GOURMET—MEALS IN MINUTES cookbook, you and your family can enjoy a delicious meal any night of the week, however hectic your day.

These recipes were created with you in mind. Most can be prepared in 30 minutes or less. Some are designed to be prepared ahead and served later. Many use the microwave oven, making the cooking quicker-than-quick. And to make your complete dinner even easier, we've included suggestions with each recipe for presenting them with style. Plus you'll find dozens of time-saving hints.

Within an hour, you can serve up wonderful dishes like Vegetable Confetti Stuffed Chicken or Hot 'n' Spicy Broccoli Beef. With little effort, surprise your kids with Mexican Lasagna or Vegetables Roma. Last minute guests? Take a look at our Casual Entertaining Menu on page 82. There you'll find everything you need to put together a great dinner that everyone will enjoy.

What makes these recipes so easy to prepare and yet so flavorful are Lawry's products—from our foil-packaged Seasoning Blends such as Extra Rich & Thick Spaghetti Sauce and Taco Seasoning Blend, to our quality Spice Blends such as our famous Seasoned Salt, Lemon Pepper Seasoning and Garlic Powder with Parsley.

We hope you find the WEEKDAY GOURMET cookbook a valuable source of cooking ideas that you'll refer to again and again. And we would appreciate your comments or questions concerning this cookbook. Just fill out the card at the back of the book and send it to us; or call us, toll-free, at 1-800-9-LAWRYS, weekdays 8 AM to 5 PM P.S.T.

PANTRY LIST

To be a Weekday Gourmet, a well-stocked pantry is a must! The following supply list will prepare you for those spur-of-the-moment meals when a trip to the grocery store is out of the question.

FREEZER
  1 package (10 ounces) frozen mixed vegetables
  1 package (6 ounces) frozen Chinese pea pods
  1 pound ground beef or turkey
  1 pound boneless chicken breasts
  1 package (10 ounces) frozen spinach
  1 package (10 ounces) frozen cut broccoli
  1 pound Cheddar cheese
  1 pound mozzarella or Monterey Jack cheese
  ½ pound Parmesan cheese (block, not grated)
  1 dozen tortillas
  Frozen orange juice concentrate

STAPLES
  Pasta—two or three varieties, such as fettuccine, bow-tie macaroni or mostaccioli
  1 package (2 pounds) long-grain rice
  1 can (6 ounces) tuna or chicken
  2 cans (4 ounces each) diced green chiles
  1 can (2.2 ounces) sliced pitted black olives
  2 cans (4 ounces each) sliced mushrooms
  2 cans (8¾ ounces each) whole kernel corn
  1 can (16 ounces) refried beans
  1 can (14½ ounces) chicken broth
  1 can (10¾ ounces) condensed cream of mushroom soup

  1 can (8 ounces) unseasoned dry bread crumbs
  2 cans (6 ounces each) tomato paste
  2 cans (8 ounces each) tomato sauce
  2 cans (14½ ounces each) whole tomatoes
  1 bottle (12 ounces) red wine vinegar
  1 bottle (24 ounces) vegetable oil
  1 bottle (12 ounces) salsa
  1 bottle (3 ounces) Lawry's Seasoned Salt
  1 bottle (1.62 ounces) Lawry's Seasoned Pepper
  1 bottle (2.87 ounces) Lawry's Lemon Pepper Seasoning
  1 bottle (3.25 ounces) Lawry's Garlic Powder with Parsley
  1 bottle (3 ounces) Lawry's Garlic Salt
  1 package (1.25 ounces) Lawry's Taco Seasoning Mix
  1 package (1.5 ounces) Lawry's Spaghetti Sauce Seasoning Blend with Imported Mushrooms
  1 package (1.5 ounces) Lawry's Extra Rich & Thick Spaghetti Sauce Seasoning Blend

FANCY EXTRAS
  1 can (8¾ ounces) miniature corn
  1 jar (8 ounces) Dijon mustard
  1 jar (3¼ ounces) capers
  1 jar (2 ounces) diced pimiento
  A variety of nuts, such as chopped walnuts, almonds and pecans
  Wooden skewers

ENTRÉES

Main dishes are a snap with these time-saving recipes and tips. Most call for easy-to-use ingredients, such as pre-trimmed cuts of meat and poultry, quick-cooking pastas and Lawry's Seasoning and Spice Blends.

BEEF & PORK

SPICY PORK

A great dish to prepare ahead of time; it also freezes well.

1 tablespoon vegetable oil
1 pound boneless pork *or* beef, cut into 1-inch cubes
1 medium onion, chopped
1 package (1.25 ounces) Lawry's Taco Seasoning Mix
¼ teaspoon Lawry's Garlic Powder with Parsley

1 can (14½ ounces) whole tomatoes, cut up
1 can (3¼ ounces) pitted ripe olives, drained
1 bay leaf
½ teaspoon hot pepper sauce (optional)

In Dutch oven, heat oil and brown pork. Add onion; cook and stir until tender and lightly browned. Add remaining ingredients; blend well. Bring to a boil. Reduce heat; cover and simmer 1 hour, stirring occasionally, until pork is tender. Uncover last 15 minutes to reduce liquid, if desired. Remove bay leaf before serving. *Makes 4 servings*

PRESENTATION: Serve over fluffy rice or with warmed corn tortillas.

NEW ORLEANS BAYOU BURGERS

The seasonings add extra zip to an all-American favorite!

1 pound lean ground beef
¼ cup thinly sliced green onions
1 teaspoon Lawry's Seasoned Salt
¾ teaspoon dried basil, crushed
½ teaspoon Lawry's Garlic Powder
    with Parsley

½ teaspoon dried thyme, crushed
½ teaspoon hot pepper sauce
4 onion rolls, split in half

In large bowl, combine all ingredients except onion rolls; blend well. Shape mixture into 4 patties. Place on broiler pan. Broil, 4 inches from heat, until desired doneness, about 15 minutes for medium-rare, turning once halfway through cooking time. Serve on onion rolls.   *Makes 4 servings*

PRESENTATION: For extra flavor, serve burgers with sautéed onions and lettuce.

HINT: Burgers are delicious when cooked over a charcoal fire.

HOT 'N' SPICY BROCCOLI BEEF

Lawry's version of a Szechwan classic.

3 tablespoons vegetable oil
1 flank *or* round steak (about
   1 pound), cut into thin strips
3 cups broccoli flowerettes
½ cup water
1 teaspoon crushed red pepper

¼ teaspoon Lawry's Garlic Powder
   with Parsley
¼ cup ketchup
1 to 2 tablespoons soy sauce
1½ teaspoons cornstarch
½ teaspoon ground ginger

In large skillet, heat oil and stir-fry steak until just browned. Remove steak and set aside. In same skillet, add broccoli, ¼ cup of the water, red pepper and Garlic Powder with Parsley. Cover and cook 5 minutes. Meanwhile, in small bowl, combine remaining ingredients; blend well. Return meat to skillet; blend in ketchup mixture. Bring to a boil. Cook until sauce thickens and glaze develops. *Makes 4 servings*

PRESENTATION: Garnish with scallions. Serve over chow mein noodles with sliced cucumbers and carrot sticks on the side.

MEAT LOAF OLÉ ▶

Turn a family favorite into a Mexican fiesta.

1½ pounds lean ground beef
¾ cup unseasoned dry bread crumbs
1 egg, beaten
1 can (4 ounces) diced green chiles
½ cup (2 ounces) grated Cheddar cheese
1 package (1.25 ounces) Lawry's Taco Seasoning Mix

1 medium tomato, chopped
½ cup sliced green onions
2 tablespoons ketchup
1 tablespoon salsa
½ teaspoon Lawry's Seasoned Salt

In large bowl, combine ground beef, bread crumbs, egg, chiles, Cheddar cheese and Taco Seasoning Mix; blend well. Pat meat mixture into 9×5×3-inch loaf pan. Bake, uncovered, in 350°F oven about 1 hour or until meat is cooked through. Let stand 10 minutes before draining fat and removing meat loaf from pan. In small bowl, combine remaining ingredients. Slice meat loaf into ½-inch slices and spoon tomato mixture over slices. *Makes 6 servings*

PRESENTATION: Serve with Mexican rice.

MUSTARD & HERB BROILED STEAK

For that special dinner for two.

1 cup Dijon mustard
2 green onions with tops, minced
2½ teaspoons dried basil, crushed
1 teaspoon Lawry's Garlic Powder with Parsley

1 teaspoon Lawry's Seasoned Salt
1 top sirloin steak (1½ to 2 pounds), cut 1½ inches thick
3 tablespoons dry white wine

In small bowl, combine mustard, onions and seasonings; blend well. Pierce steak 4 times with fork. Spread mixture on both sides of steak, reserving extra. Place steak on broiler pan. Broil, 4 inches from heat, until desired doneness, about 10 minutes on each side for medium. Brush steak with some of the reserved mustard mixture before serving. In small saucepan, combine remaining mustard mixture and wine. Heat until warmed through. Use for dipping or pour over sliced steak. *Makes 2 servings*

PRESENTATION: Serve with spinach soufflé and a marinated tomato, onion and cucumber salad.

PORK CHOPS WITH CREOLE SAUCE

A red sauce with real kick!

1 package (1.5 ounces) Lawry's Extra Rich & Thick Spaghetti Sauce Seasoning Blend
1 can (6 ounces) tomato paste
1¾ cups water
2 tablespoons butter or vegetable oil
1 can (4 ounces) sliced mushrooms, finely chopped
1 green bell pepper, finely chopped
½ to 1 teaspoon hot red pepper sauce
¼ teaspoon celery seed
4 to 6 pork chops (about 4 ounces each)

In medium saucepan, prepare Extra Rich & Thick Spaghetti Sauce Seasoning Blend according to package directions with tomato paste, water and butter. Add mushrooms, green pepper, pepper sauce and celery seed. In large, nonstick skillet, pan-fry pork chops 10 to 12 minutes, depending on thickness of chops, until pork is no longer pink. Top with prepared sauce.

Makes 4 to 6 servings

PRESENTATION: Serve with oven-browned potatoes and steamed sliced zucchini.

MEXICAN LASAGNA

This hearty dish uses tortillas in place of lasagna noodles with a sauce that adds extra zip!

1½ pounds lean ground beef
1 package (1.25 ounces) Lawry's Taco Seasoning Mix
1 teaspoon Lawry's Seasoned Salt
1 cup diced tomatoes, fresh or canned
2 cans (8 ounces each) tomato sauce
1 can (4 ounces) diced green chiles
1 cup ricotta cheese
2 eggs, beaten
10 corn tortillas
2½ cups (10 ounces) grated Monterey Jack cheese

In large skillet, brown ground beef, stirring until cooked through; drain fat. Add Taco Seasoning Mix, Seasoned Salt, tomatoes, tomato sauce and chiles; blend well. Bring to a boil. Reduce heat; simmer, uncovered, 10 minutes. In small bowl, combine ricotta cheese and eggs. In bottom of 13×9×2-inch baking dish, spread ½ of meat mixture. Top with ½ of tortillas; spread ½ of ricotta cheese mixture over tortillas and top with ½ of grated Monterey Jack cheese. Repeat layering, ending with grated cheese. Bake, uncovered, in 350°F oven 20 to 30 minutes or until hot and bubbly. Let stand 10 minutes before cutting into squares. *Makes 8 servings*

PRESENTATION: Serve with a lettuce, orange and red onion salad.

HINTS: You may assemble the lasagna early in the day and refrigerate it, covered, until ready to bake. Add 10 to 15 minutes to baking time. Mexican Lasagna also freezes well; defrost completely before baking.

SPECIAL SAN FRANCISCO PITA POCKET ▶

A great sandwich for lunch or brunch.

1 package (10 ounces) frozen
chopped spinach
¾ pound lean ground beef
½ pound fresh mushrooms, sliced
½ cup chopped onion
3 tablespoons butter or margarine
¾ teaspoon dill weed
½ teaspoon Lawry's Seasoned Salt

½ teaspoon Lawry's Garlic Powder
with Parsley
½ teaspoon Lawry's Seasoned
Pepper
2 cups (8 ounces) grated cheese
(½ Cheddar and ½ Monterey
Jack)
4 pita breads, cut in half

MICROWAVE DIRECTIONS: Make slit in spinach package; place package, slit side up, on paper towel. Microwave on HIGH 5 minutes. Remove spinach from package; squeeze liquid from spinach. In microwave-safe pie plate or dish, microwave ground beef on HIGH 6 to 7 minutes, stirring once or twice. Drain fat. In 13×9×2-inch microwave-safe baking dish, microwave mushrooms, onion and butter on HIGH 8 to 10 minutes. Stir in seasonings. Microwave on HIGH 3 minutes, stirring once. Stir spinach and cooked ground beef into mushroom-onion mixture. Fold in cheese. Cover with waxed paper and microwave on HIGH 3 minutes. Wrap pita breads loosely in plastic wrap; microwave on HIGH 30 seconds to warm. Open pita breads and fill with meat mixture. Serve immediately.   *Makes 8 servings*

PRESENTATION: Serve with assorted fresh fruit.

HINT: Ground turkey can be substituted for ground beef. Microwave on HIGH 4 to 5 minutes, stirring twice.

PORK EL DORADO

A hearty and delicious filling for burritos.

1 pound ground pork
1 can (4 ounces) diced green chiles

1 package (1.25 ounces) Lawry's
Taco Seasoning Mix
¾ cup water

In large skillet, brown pork, stirring, until cooked through; drain fat. Stir in chiles, Taco Seasoning Mix and water; blend well. Bring to a boil. Reduce heat; simmer, uncovered, 5 to 10 minutes.   *Makes 4 to 6 servings*

PRESENTATION: Serve in warm flour tortillas, rolled up, topped with dairy sour cream. Or serve over Mexican rice.

ONE-SKILLET SWISS STEAK

A quick and easy version of a traditional family favorite.

3 tablespoons all-purpose flour
1 teaspoon Lawry's Seasoned Salt
¾ teaspoon Lawry's Seasoned
   Pepper
1 boneless round steak (about
   1½ pounds)
3 tablespoons vegetable oil
1 can (14½ ounces) whole
   tomatoes, cut up

1 medium onion, thinly sliced
1 teaspoon Lawry's Garlic Powder
   with Parsley
1 can (8¾ ounces) whole kernel
   corn
½ cup chopped green bell pepper

In pie plate, combine flour, Seasoned Salt and Seasoned Pepper; coat steak with flour mixture. In large skillet, heat oil and brown steak on both sides. Add tomatoes, onion and Garlic Powder with Parsley. Bring to a boil. Reduce heat; cover and simmer 25 minutes. Add corn and green pepper; cover and simmer 15 minutes longer. *Makes 4 servings*

PRESENTATION: Serve with mashed potatoes or cooked egg noodles.

PORK LOIN WITH RAISIN STUFFING

A perfect combination of flavors.

1⅔ cups water
1 package (6 ounces) stuffing mix
1 cup raisins
¼ cup dry sherry wine (optional)
¼ cup slivered almonds
1 teaspoon ground cinnamon

½ teaspoon Lawry's Garlic Powder
   with Parsley
2 tablespoons olive or vegetable oil
3 pounds boneless pork tenderloin,
   cut into 8 to 10 slices
Lawry's Seasoned Pepper

In medium saucepan, bring water to a boil; add stuffing mix, raisins, sherry, almonds, cinnamon and Garlic Powder with Parsley. Remove from heat and let stand 20 minutes. Meanwhile, in large skillet, heat oil and sauté pork slices 2 to 3 minutes on each side until pork is no longer pink. Sprinkle with Seasoned Pepper to taste. *Makes 4 to 6 servings*

PRESENTATION: Serve stuffing and pork slices with apple slices.

POULTRY

GRILLED ORANGE CHICKEN

A zesty citrus-flavored chicken dish.

1 pound boneless chicken breasts,
  skinned
1 teaspoon grated orange peel
½ cup orange juice
1 tablespoon vegetable oil

2 teaspoons Worcestershire sauce
1 teaspoon Lawry's Lemon Pepper
  Seasoning
Lawry's Garlic Salt

With sharp knife, score chicken on both sides. Place chicken in shallow glass dish. In small bowl, combine orange peel, orange juice, oil, Worcestershire sauce and Lemon Pepper Seasoning. Pour marinade over chicken to coat. Cover and refrigerate 30 minutes to 1 hour. Remove chicken from marinade; reserve marinade. Sprinkle both sides of chicken with Garlic Salt to taste. Grill chicken over medium-hot coals 10 to 15 minutes or until tender and cooked through, basting once with reserved marinade. *Makes 4 servings*

PRESENTATION: Garnish each serving with an orange slice and red onion slice.

PECAN TURKEY SAUTÉ WITH WARM CRANBERRY SAUCE

A quick and easy recipe with a touch of holiday cheer.

½ cup unseasoned dry bread crumbs
¼ cup ground pecans
½ teaspoon Lawry's Garlic Powder
  with Parsley
½ teaspoon Lawry's Seasoned Salt
1 pound turkey cutlets
3 eggs, beaten

3 tablespoons butter or margarine
1 can (8 ounces) jellied cranberry
  sauce or whole berry cranberry
  sauce
⅓ cup French salad dressing
3 tablespoons water
2 tablespoons chopped green onion

In pie plate, combine bread crumbs, pecans and seasonings; blend well. Dip each turkey cutlet in eggs, then coat both sides with crumb mixture. In large skillet, melt butter and brown turkey cutlets 5 minutes on each side or until cooked through. In small saucepan, combine cranberry sauce, salad dressing, water and onion; blend well. Gently heat until warmed through, about 5 minutes. Spoon warm cranberry sauce over cutlets. *Makes 4 servings*

PRESENTATION: Serve with mashed potatoes or stuffing.

ROAST GARLIC CHICKEN ▶

Garlic powder adds great flavor to this easy-to-prepare chicken dish.

1 whole broiler/fryer chicken (2 to 3 pounds)	1½ teaspoons Lawry's Garlic Powder with Parsley
2 tablespoons lemon juice	1 teaspoon Lawry's Seasoned Salt

Sprinkle chicken with lemon juice, Garlic Powder with Parsley and Seasoned Salt. Wrap chicken loosely in foil. Refrigerate overnight. Place chicken in large baking dish and bake, uncovered, in 375°F oven 1 hour or until chicken is tender and juices run clear when tested with a fork in thigh.

Makes 4 servings

PRESENTATION: Garnish with lemon slices and fresh sage leaves. Serve with homemade biscuits and honey.

CRISPY SKILLET TURKEY

A quick, no-bake casserole, sure to be a hit!

½ cup seasoned dry bread crumbs	1 small onion, diced
¾ pound turkey cutlets, cut into bite-size pieces	2 cups sliced fresh mushrooms
1 egg, beaten	½ teaspoon Lawry's Seasoned Salt
¼ cup plus 2 tablespoons olive or vegetable oil	½ teaspoon Lawry's Seasoned Pepper
2 large carrots, cut diagonally into ¼-inch slices	Large bunch fresh spinach leaves
	Parmesan cheese

In shallow dish, place bread crumbs. Dip turkey pieces in egg, then coat with bread crumbs. In large skillet, heat ¼ cup oil and pan-fry turkey until golden. Remove from skillet and keep warm. Wipe out skillet; add remaining 2 tablespoons oil. Add carrots and onion; cook and stir 5 minutes or until onion is transparent. Stir in mushrooms, Seasoned Salt and Seasoned Pepper; heat 5 minutes. Add spinach and heat just until wilted. Add turkey; sprinkle with Parmesan cheese.

Makes 4 servings

PRESENTATION: Serve with sliced tomatoes and homemade biscuits.

HINT: Any leftover meat, such as cooked roast beef or corned beef, can be substituted for the pan-fried turkey. Stir in meat as directed.

ORANGE-HONEY GLAZED CHICKEN

Highlight your next dinner with this fragrant, tangy dish.

½ cup unseasoned dry bread crumbs
1 pound boneless chicken breasts,
  halved and skinned
3 tablespoons vegetable oil
¾ cup orange juice
2 tablespoons honey
2 teaspoons Dijon mustard

1 teaspoon cornstarch
½ teaspoon Lawry's Garlic Powder
  with Parsley
½ teaspoon Lawry's Seasoned Salt
½ teaspoon dried tarragon, crushed
1 medium onion, thinly sliced and
  separated into rings

In pie plate, place bread crumbs; coat chicken. In large skillet, heat oil and brown chicken on both sides. In small bowl, combine remaining ingredients except onion; blend well. Pour over chicken; add onion. Bring to a boil. Reduce heat; simmer, uncovered, 25 minutes or until chicken is tender and cooked through. Baste with sauce occasionally. *Makes 4 servings*

PRESENTATION: Serve with seasoned rice or pasta.

ORIENTAL ALMOND CHICKEN

A quick-and-easy stir-fry.

1¼ cups chicken broth
2 tablespoons soy sauce
3 tablespoons cornstarch
1 teaspoon Lawry's Garlic Powder
   with Parsley
2 tablespoons vegetable oil
1 pound boneless chicken breasts,
   skinned and cut into cubes

1 can (5 ounces) sliced water
   chestnuts, drained
8 to 10 green onions, cut diagonally
   into 1-inch pieces
1 cup diagonally sliced celery
¾ cup slivered almonds

In small bowl, combine chicken broth, soy sauce, cornstarch and Garlic Powder with Parsley; blend well. In large skillet or wok, heat oil and stir-fry chicken 5 to 7 minutes or until browned. Add soy sauce mixture to chicken along with water chestnuts, green onions and celery. Stir-fry until vegetables are crisp-tender and sauce has thickened. Stir in almonds. *Makes 4 servings*

PRESENTATION: Serve with hot cooked rice. For a refreshing dessert, try orange slices sprinkled with shredded coconut.

MEXICAN MONTEREY CHICKEN

A new twist on chicken breasts: filled with cheese
and chiles and baked in a crisp coating.

2 pounds boneless chicken breasts,
   halved and skinned
4 ounces Monterey Jack cheese, cut
   into 6 slices
1 can (4 ounces) diced green chiles,
   drained

2 cups crushed Cheddar cheese
   crackers
1 package (1.25 ounces) Lawry's
   Taco Seasoning Mix

Place chicken breasts between 2 sheets of waxed paper; pound with meat mallet or rolling pin to flatten. Place 1 slice of Monterey Jack cheese and 1 tablespoon of chiles on each breast; wrap breasts around filling and secure with wooden toothpicks. In shallow dish, combine crackers and Taco Seasoning Mix; blend well. Add chicken bundles; press crumbs onto chicken to coat. Place bundles in greased 9×9×2-inch baking dish. Bake in 350°F oven 20 to 30 minutes or until chicken is tender. *Makes 4 to 6 servings*

PRESENTATION: Serve with Mexican rice.

HINT: For spicier flavor, substitute hot pepper cheese for Monterey Jack.

TURKEY PARMIGIANA ▶

A gourmet dish that's oh-so-quick to prepare!

1 package (1.5 ounces) Lawry's
Extra Rich & Thick Spaghetti
Sauce Seasoning Blend
1 can (6 ounces) tomato paste
1¾ cups water
4 tablespoons butter or vegetable
oil

½ cup unseasoned dry bread crumbs
½ cup grated Parmesan cheese
1 pound sliced turkey cutlets
1 egg, beaten
1 cup (4 ounces) grated mozzarella
cheese

In medium saucepan, prepare Extra Rich & Thick Spaghetti Sauce Seasoning Blend according to package directions with tomato paste, water and 2 tablespoons of the butter. In pie plate, combine bread crumbs and ¼ cup of the Parmesan cheese. Dip each turkey cutlet in beaten egg, then coat with crumb mixture. In large skillet, heat remaining 2 tablespoons butter and brown turkey on both sides. Place in 12×8×2-inch baking dish; top with prepared spaghetti sauce. Sprinkle with mozzarella and remaining ¼ cup Parmesan cheese. Bake, covered, in 350°F oven 25 minutes or until hot and bubbly.

Makes 4 to 6 servings

PRESENTATION: Serve with crusty Italian rolls or garlic bread and a green salad.

HINT: 1 pound boneless chicken breasts, skinned and flattened, or veal cutlets can be substituted for the turkey.

ALL-AMERICAN FRIED CHICKEN

A picnic favorite.

½ cup all-purpose flour
1 to 2 teaspoons Lawry's Seasoned
Salt

1 to 2 teaspoons Lawry's Seasoned
Pepper
2½ to 3 pounds chicken pieces
Vegetable oil

In plastic bag, combine flour, Seasoned Salt and Seasoned Pepper. Wash chicken pieces; pat dry with paper towels. Place chicken pieces, a few at a time, in flour mixture. Seal bag and shake to coat. In large skillet, pour ½ inch oil. Heat oil and brown chicken, a few pieces at a time. Remove to baking dish. When all chicken is browned, bake chicken, covered, in 350°F oven 30 minutes or until chicken is tender and juices run clear when tested with fork. For crispy skin, uncover during last 10 minutes of baking.

Makes 4 servings

PRESENTATION: Serve in napkin-lined basket. Place layer of plastic wrap over napkin to protect it from oil stains.

HINT: For a unique flavor twist, add 1½ teaspoons ground cinnamon to flour mixture. Proceed as directed.

VEGETABLE CONFETTI STUFFED CHICKEN ▶

A great tasting dish that's as appealing to the eye as it is to the palate.

1½ pounds boneless chicken breasts, skinned
1 tablespoon vegetable oil
1 carrot, cut into julienne strips
1 zucchini, cut into julienne strips
1 red bell pepper, cut into julienne strips
½ teaspoon Lawry's Seasoned Salt

¼ teaspoon Lawry's Garlic Powder with Parsley
4 ounces Cheddar cheese, thinly sliced
½ cup dry white wine *or* chicken broth
Lawry's Seasoned Salt
Lawry's Lemon Pepper Seasoning

Place chicken breasts between 2 sheets of waxed paper; pound with meat mallet or rolling pin to flatten to ¼-inch thickness. In medium skillet, heat oil and sauté carrot, zucchini and red pepper with ½ teaspoon Seasoned Salt and Garlic Powder with Parsley. On each chicken breast, place 1 slice of Cheddar cheese. Divide vegetable mixture evenly among chicken breasts. Roll up each breast and secure with wooden toothpicks.

MICROWAVE DIRECTIONS: Place chicken rolls in microwave-safe dish; pour wine over rolls. Cover with vented plastic wrap and microwave on HIGH 8 to 12 minutes or until chicken is cooked through. Let stand 5 minutes. Drain off excess liquid. Sprinkle with Seasoned Salt and Lemon Pepper Seasoning to taste. *Makes 6 servings*

PRESENTATION: Slice chicken rolls into ¼-inch slices. Serve with seasoned rice and garnish with tomato rose.

CHICKEN 'N' RICE PICANTE

A one-skillet meal with a Mexican twist — sure to become a family favorite.

¼ cup all-purpose flour
¾ teaspoon Lawry's Seasoned Salt
1 pound boneless chicken breasts, skinned and cut into cubes
2 tablespoons vegetable oil
2 cans (14½ ounces each) whole tomatoes, cut up
1 package (1.25 ounces) Lawry's Taco Seasoning Mix

1 cup thinly sliced celery
½ cup chopped onion
1 can (2.2 ounces) sliced pitted ripe olives
1 cup uncooked long-grain rice
1 cup water
½ cup (2 ounces) grated Cheddar cheese

In plastic bag, combine flour and Seasoned Salt. Add chicken. Seal bag and shake to coat. In large skillet, heat oil and brown chicken, stirring occasionally. Add remaining ingredients except cheese; blend well. Bring to a boil. Reduce heat; cover and simmer 25 to 30 minutes or until liquid is absorbed and rice is tender. Sprinkle with Cheddar cheese. *Makes 4 to 6 servings*

PRESENTATION: Serve with steamed fresh vegetables and a fruit juice cooler.

SEAFOOD

TUNA CRUZ MELT ▶

A Mexican-flavored version of the classic Tuna Melt.

1 can (12½ ounces) water-packed
   white tuna, drained
1 can (4 ounces) diced green chiles,
   drained
1 can (2.2 ounces) sliced pitted ripe
   olives, drained

¼ cup mayonnaise
½ teaspoon Lawry's Seasoned Salt
4 flour tortillas
1 cup (4 ounces) grated Cheddar
   cheese
1 green onion with top, chopped

In medium bowl, flake tuna. Add chiles, olives, mayonnaise and Seasoned Salt; blend well. Spoon ¼ of mixture onto each tortilla. Top with equal portions of Cheddar cheese. Place on broiler pan and broil, 4 inches from heat, until cheese is hot and bubbly. Sprinkle each tortilla with green onion.

Makes 4 servings

PRESENTATION: Garnish each serving with parsley. Serve open face or fold over, soft-taco style.

SESAME BAKED FISH

Toasted sesame seeds provide crunch and a tasty flavor.

½ cup milk
1 tablespoon Dijon mustard
½ cup unseasoned dry bread crumbs
¼ to ½ cup sesame seeds, lightly
   toasted
1 teaspoon dried tarragon, crushed
1 teaspoon Lawry's Lemon Pepper
   Seasoning

½ teaspoon Lawry's Seasoned Salt
¼ teaspoon Lawry's Garlic Powder
   with Parsley
4 fresh white fish fillets (about
   1 pound)

In shallow dish, combine milk and mustard; blend well. In pie plate, combine bread crumbs, sesame seeds and seasonings. Wash fillets; pat dry with paper towels. Dip each fillet in milk mixture, then coat in sesame seed mixture. Place on broiler pan. Bake in 400°F oven 10 to 15 minutes or until fish begins to flake when tested with a fork.

Makes 4 servings

PRESENTATION: Garnish with lemon wedges and fresh parsley. Serve with fresh steamed vegetables and baked potatoes.

PRIZE CATCH SWORDFISH

A tantalizing main dish to serve to guests.

1 medium tomato, chopped
1 cup sliced fresh mushrooms
1 small red onion, diced
1 green bell pepper, diced
1½ pounds swordfish steaks

Olive or vegetable oil
Lawry's Garlic Salt
Lawry's Seasoned Pepper
4 ounces feta cheese, crumbled

In medium bowl, combine tomato, mushrooms, onion and green pepper. Wash swordfish steaks; pat dry with paper towels. Cut steaks into 4 equal pieces; measure fish at its thickest part to determine cooking time. Rub each piece with oil; season with Garlic Salt and Seasoned Pepper to taste. Tear off 4 pieces of parchment paper or aluminum foil, 12×8 inches each. Fold each piece of paper in half lengthwise; open flat. Place 1 piece of fish on right side of fold. Spoon vegetables over fish. Fold left side of paper over fish; crimp edges together to form tight seal. Place packets on jelly-roll pan or baking sheet. Bake in 350°F oven about 10 minutes per inch of thickness of fish. Transfer packets to individual serving plates. Just before serving, open packets and sprinkle each serving with feta cheese. *Makes 4 servings*

PRESENTATION: Serve with a fresh cucumber salad.

MICROWAVE DIRECTIONS: Wrap fish in parchment paper *(do not use aluminum foil)*. Microwave sealed packets on HIGH 6 to 8 minutes, rotating half a turn every 2 minutes of cooking time.

CAJUN SPICY SHRIMP

An easy Cajun-style dish for entertaining in a hurry.

¼ cup butter or margarine
¼ cup dry white wine
1 teaspoon Lawry's Garlic Salt
½ teaspoon dried rosemary, crushed
½ teaspoon paprika

¼ teaspoon dried basil, crushed
¼ to ½ teaspoon dried oregano,
   crushed
1 pound fresh large shrimp, peeled
   and deveined with tails left on

In large skillet, melt butter; add white wine and seasonings. Bring to a boil. Reduce heat; simmer, uncovered, 5 minutes. Wash shrimp; pat dry with paper towels. Add to skillet and sauté until shrimp turn pink.

Makes 4 to 6 servings

PRESENTATION: Serve over hot cooked rice or spaghetti.

LEMON CATFISH BAKE ▶

Lemon and dill team up to give perfect flavor to these fillets.

2 tablespoons butter or margarine, melted
2 tablespoons lemon juice
¼ cup unseasoned dry bread crumbs
¾ teaspoon Lawry's Lemon Pepper Seasoning

½ teaspoon Lawry's Seasoned Salt
¼ teaspoon dill weed
4 fresh catfish fillets or other white fish fillets (about 1 pound)
Paprika

In pie plate, combine butter and lemon juice; set aside. In another pie plate, combine bread crumbs, Lemon Pepper Seasoning, Seasoned Salt and dill weed. Wash fillets; pat dry with paper towels. Dip each fillet in butter mixture, then in bread crumb mixture. Place in ungreased 12×8×2-inch baking dish. Pour remaining butter mixture over fillets; sprinkle lightly with paprika. Bake, uncovered, in 350°F oven 25 to 30 minutes or until fish begins to flake when tested with a fork.   *Makes 4 servings*

PRESENTATION: Garnish with lemon slices and fresh dill. Serve with fresh steamed vegetables, potatoes or rice.

ORANGE ROUGHY AU GRATIN

A fish dish the whole family will enjoy.

4 orange roughy fillets (about 1 pound)
1 tablespoon butter or margarine
2 tablespoons diced celery
4 green onions, cut into ½-inch pieces
2 teaspoons all-purpose flour

½ teaspoon Lawry's Seasoned Salt
½ teaspoon Lawry's Seasoned Pepper
⅓ cup milk
½ cup (2 ounces) grated Swiss cheese

Wash fillets; pat dry with paper towels. Place fillets in 10×6×2-inch greased baking dish. In small skillet, melt butter and sauté celery and onions 5 minutes. Stir in flour, Seasoned Salt and Seasoned Pepper; cook 1 minute. Gradually blend in milk and Swiss cheese. Cook until cheese is melted. Pour mixture over fillets. Cover and bake in 350°F oven 25 minutes or until fish begins to flake when tested with a fork. Carefully drain off excess liquid.

Makes 4 servings

PRESENTATION: Garnish with chopped parsley. Serve with boiled potatoes.

MICROWAVE DIRECTIONS: Place fillets in microwave-safe 10×6×2-inch baking dish. Microwave on HIGH 4 minutes; drain. Prepare sauce as directed; pour over fillets. Cover with vented plastic wrap and microwave on HIGH 3 to 5 minutes longer or until fish begins to flake when tested with a fork. Carefully drain off excess liquid.

MARINATED SCALLOPS EN BROCHETTE ▶

A delectable way to serve scallops.

½ cup butter or margarine, melted
¼ cup dry vermouth
¼ cup orange juice concentrate
1 tablespoon honey
1 tablespoon minced parsley
1 teaspoon Lawry's Lemon Pepper Seasoning
½ teaspoon dill weed
½ teaspoon dried basil, crushed
¼ teaspoon Lawry's Garlic Powder with Parsley
30 small fresh sea scallops, rinsed and drained
½ pound bacon, cut into 2-inch pieces
3 to 4 limes, cut into thin slices

In shallow glass dish, combine butter, vermouth, orange juice concentrate, honey, parsley and seasonings. Add scallops; cover and refrigerate at least 1 hour. Thread scallops, bacon and lime slices alternately onto metal skewers. Place skewers on broiler rack and broil, 4 inches from heat, 3 to 5 minutes on each side, basting frequently with marinade, until scallops turn opaque.

Makes 5 to 6 servings

PRESENTATION: Serve on a bed of rice pilaf.

RED SNAPPER VERA CRUZ

Olives, chiles and tomatoes give this dish a lively flair.

4 fresh red snapper fillets (about 1 pound)
Lemon juice
Lawry's Seasoned Salt
Lawry's Seasoned Pepper
3 tablespoons vegetable oil
½ cup chopped onion
½ teaspoon Lawry's Garlic Powder with Parsley
1 can (14½ ounces) whole tomatoes, cut up
¼ cup sliced pimiento-stuffed green olives
2 tablespoons diced green chiles

Rub fish with lemon juice; sprinkle with Seasoned Salt and Seasoned Pepper to taste. In medium skillet, heat oil; gently sauté fish 1 minute on each side. Remove to baking dish. In same skillet, sauté onion and Garlic Powder with Parsley. Add tomatoes and Seasoned Pepper to taste. Bring to a boil. Reduce heat; simmer, uncovered, 20 minutes, stirring occasionally. Top fish with olives and chiles; pour sauce over all. Bake, uncovered, in 300°F oven 30 minutes or until fish begins to flake when tested with a fork. *Makes 4 servings*

PRESENTATION: Garnish with chopped parsley. Serve with cooked rice and steamed broccoli.

LIGHT ENTRÉES

SINGAPORE SPICY NOODLES ▶

A pasta dish with a taste of the Orient.

1¼ cups water
2 tablespoons ketchup
2½ teaspoons packed brown sugar
1½ teaspoons chopped cilantro
1 teaspoon cornstarch
¾ teaspoon Lawry's Seasoned Salt
¾ teaspoon Lawry's Garlic Powder
  with Parsley

¼ teaspoon crushed red pepper
2½ tablespoons chunky peanut butter
¼ cup sliced green onions
8 ounces linguine, cooked and
  drained
1 cup shredded red cabbage

In medium saucepan, combine water, ketchup, sugar, cilantro, cornstarch and seasonings. Bring to a boil. Reduce heat; simmer, uncovered, 5 minutes. Cool 10 minutes; blend in peanut butter and green onions. Toss sauce with hot linguine and red cabbage. *Makes 4 servings*

PRESENTATION: Garnish with green onion curls. Serve with a marinated cucumber salad.

HINT: For a heartier entrée, add cooked shredded chicken or pork.

GARLIC PARMESAN PASTA

A dish with robust flavor that's also quick and convenient to prepare.

½ cup butter or margarine
2 teaspoons dried basil, crushed
2 teaspoons lemon juice
1¼ teaspoons Lawry's Garlic Powder
  with Parsley
¾ teaspoon Lawry's Seasoned Salt
8 ounces fettuccine, cooked and
  drained

1½ cups broccoli flowerettes, cooked
  tender-crisp
3 tablespoons chopped walnuts
½ cup grated Parmesan or Romano
  cheese

In large skillet, melt butter. Add basil, lemon juice, Garlic Powder with Parsley and Seasoned Salt; blend well. Add fettuccine, broccoli, walnuts and Parmesan cheese; toss to coat. *Makes 4 servings*

PRESENTATION: Serve with a fresh spinach salad.

PIZZA PASTA

The taste of pizza in a family-pleasing casserole.

4 ounces thinly sliced pepperoni
1 medium green bell pepper,
  chopped
1 medium onion, chopped
1 cup sliced fresh mushrooms
1 package (1.5 ounces) Lawry's
  Extra Rich & Thick Spaghetti
  Sauce Seasoning Blend

1 can (6 ounces) tomato paste
1¾ cups water
2 tablespoons vegetable oil
8 ounces mostaccioli, cooked and
  drained
1 cup (4 ounces) grated mozzarella
  cheese

In large skillet, brown pepperoni; drain fat. Add green pepper, onion and mushrooms; sauté 5 minutes. Add Extra Rich & Thick Spaghetti Sauce Seasoning Blend, tomato paste, water and oil; blend well. Bring to a boil. Reduce heat; simmer, uncovered, 10 minutes. Add cooked mostaccioli; blend well. Pour into 12×8×2-inch casserole; top with mozzarella cheese. Bake, uncovered, in 350°F oven 15 minutes or until cheese is melted. *Makes 6 servings*

PRESENTATION: Garnish with green pepper slices and additional pepperoni. Serve with a fresh green salad and bread sticks.

HINT: Any similar kind of cooked pasta, such as shell or elbow macaroni, can be substituted for the mostaccioli.

MUSHROOM FRITTATA

The perfect late night supper.

1 teaspoon butter or margarine
1 medium zucchini, shredded
1 medium tomato, chopped
1 can (4 ounces) sliced mushrooms,
   drained
6 eggs, beaten
¼ cup milk

2 teaspoons Dijon mustard
½ teaspoon Lawry's Seasoned Salt
½ teaspoon Lawry's Seasoned
   Pepper
2 cups (8 ounces) grated Swiss
   cheese

In large, ovenproof skillet, melt butter and sauté zucchini, tomato and mushrooms 1 minute. In large bowl, combine remaining ingredients; blend well. Pour egg mixture into skillet; cook 10 minutes over low heat. To brown top, place skillet under broiler 2 to 3 minutes.   *Makes 4 servings*

PRESENTATION: Serve directly from skillet or remove frittata to serving dish. Serve with additional Swiss cheese and fresh fruit.

HINT: Try serving frittata with prepared Lawry's Spaghetti Sauce Seasoning Blend with Imported Mushrooms.

TURKEY-SPINACH MANICOTTI ▶

A make-ahead dish to freeze for when you're too busy to cook.

1 package (1.5 ounces) Lawry's
  Spaghetti Sauce Seasoning
  Blend with Imported
  Mushrooms
1 can (28 ounces) whole tomatoes,
  cut up
1 can (8 ounces) tomato sauce
¼ cup chopped green onions
1 cup ricotta cheese
2 cups chopped fresh spinach

2 cups cooked, minced turkey or
  chicken
2 tablespoons milk
1 teaspoon Lawry's Seasoned
  Pepper
½ teaspoon Lawry's Garlic Powder
  with Parsley
8 manicotti shells, cooked and
  drained
⅓ cup grated Parmesan cheese

In medium saucepan, combine Spaghetti Sauce Seasoning Blend with Imported Mushrooms, tomatoes, tomato sauce and onions. Bring to a boil. Reduce heat; cover and simmer 20 minutes, stirring occasionally. In medium bowl, combine ricotta cheese, spinach, turkey, milk, Seasoned Pepper and Garlic Powder with Parsley; blend well. Carefully spoon mixture into manicotti shells. Pour ½ of sauce in bottom of 12×8×2-inch baking dish. Place stuffed shells on top of sauce; pour remaining sauce over shells. Cover and bake in 375°F oven 30 minutes or until heated through. Sprinkle with Parmesan cheese.

Makes 4 to 8 servings

PRESENTATION: Sprinkle with chopped parsley. Garnish with fresh basil leaves.

HINT: 1 package (10 ounces) frozen chopped spinach, thawed and drained, can be substituted for the fresh spinach.

FANCY TUXEDO ZUCCHINI PASTA

For an impressive-looking dish, try serving this bow-tie pasta recipe.

2 tablespoons butter or margarine
4 small zucchini, cut into 1½-inch
  julienne strips
1 small onion, chopped
2 carrots, cut into julienne strips or
  diced
½ teaspoon Lawry's Garlic Powder
  with Parsley

½ teaspoon all-purpose flour
¾ cup milk
 8 ounces bow-tie pasta, cooked and
  drained
⅓ cup grated Parmesan cheese
¾ teaspoon Lawry's Seasoned Salt
½ teaspoon dried basil, crushed
  Lawry's Seasoned Pepper

In large skillet, melt butter and sauté zucchini until tender, about 5 minutes. Remove and set aside. In same skillet, sauté onion, carrots and Garlic Powder with Parsley 3 minutes. Stir in flour; gradually stir in milk and boil 1 minute. Add pasta, Parmesan cheese, Seasoned Salt, basil and Seasoned Pepper to taste. Add zucchini; heat through.

Makes 4 to 6 servings

PRESENTATION: Serve with crispy garlic bread.

PASTA ROLL-UPS

A great recipe you can prepare in a snap!

1 package (1.5 ounces) Lawry's Spaghetti Sauce Seasoning Blend with Imported Mushrooms
1 can (6 ounces) tomato paste
2¼ cups water
2 tablespoons butter or vegetable oil
2 cups cottage cheese or ricotta cheese
1 cup (4 ounces) grated mozzarella cheese
¼ cup grated Parmesan cheese
2 eggs, lightly beaten
½ to 1 teaspoon Lawry's Garlic Salt
½ teaspoon dried basil, crushed (optional)
8 ounces lasagna noodles, cooked and drained

(Continued)

In medium saucepan, prepare Spaghetti Sauce Seasoning Blend with Imported Mushrooms according to package directions using tomato paste, water and butter. In large bowl, combine remaining ingredients except noodles; blend well. Spread ¼ cup cheese mixture on entire length of each lasagna noodle; roll up.

MICROWAVE DIRECTIONS: Place noodles, seam-side down, in microwave-safe baking dish. Cover with vented plastic wrap and microwave on HIGH 6 to 7 minutes or until cheese begins to melt. Pour sauce over rolls and microwave on HIGH 1 minute longer, if necessary, to heat sauce.

Makes 6 servings

PRESENTATION: Sprinkle with additional grated Parmesan cheese. Garnish with fresh basil leaves.

HINT: For quick microwaveable meals, wrap prepared rolls individually and freeze. Sauce may be frozen in ¼ cup servings.

CLAM SAUCE MARINARA

A traditional Italian sauce you can prepare in minutes.

2 tablespoons olive or vegetable oil
½ cup chopped onion
1 medium zucchini, shredded
1 package (1.5 ounces) Lawry's Extra Rich & Thick Spaghetti Sauce Seasoning Blend
1 can (6 ounces) tomato paste
1 cup water

½ teaspoon Lawry's Garlic Powder with Parsley
2 cans (8 ounces each) minced clams, drained (reserve ¾ cup clam liquid)
8 ounces linguine, cooked and drained

In medium skillet, heat oil and sauté onion and zucchini until tender, about 5 minutes. Add Extra Rich & Thick Spaghetti Sauce Seasoning Blend, tomato paste, water, Garlic Powder with Parsley and reserved clam liquid; blend well. Bring to a boil. Reduce heat; simmer, uncovered, 20 minutes, stirring occasionally. Add clams and heat 5 minutes. Toss linguine with sauce.

Makes 4 servings

PRESENTATION: Garnish with grated Parmesan cheese and chopped parsley. Serve with a Caesar salad and warmed Italian bread.

SIDE DISHES

Side dishes can be deliciously easy to prepare with just a few extra kitchen staples. Keep frozen vegetables on hand. Stock your shelves with jars of chiles and pimientos, dried fruits, nuts and Lawry's Seasonings and Seasoning Blends. Keep potatoes and rice in good supply. Suddenly, side dishes take center stage!

SALADS

CLASSIC TACO SALAD

A salad everyone will enjoy!

1 package (1.25 ounces) Lawry's
  Taco Seasoning Mix
1 pound lean ground beef
¾ cup water
4 cups shredded lettuce
1 can (15½ ounces) kidney or pinto
  beans, drained

2 medium tomatoes, cut into wedges
  Tortilla chips
½ cup chopped red or green onions
1½ cups (6 ounces) grated Cheddar
  cheese
1 can (2.2 ounces) sliced pitted ripe
  olives, drained

In large skillet, prepare Taco Seasoning Mix with ground beef and water according to package directions. Place lettuce in center of large, round platter. Mound beef mixture on top of lettuce. Spoon beans around beef mixture. Arrange tomato wedges and tortilla chips around lettuce. Sprinkle with onions, Cheddar cheese and olives.　　　　　　　　　　　　*Makes 4 to 6 servings*

PRESENTATION: Serve with guacamole or salsa and extra tortilla chips on the side.

HINTS: Shredded chicken or ground turkey can be substituted for the ground beef. For a quicker dish, prepare meat mixture as directed above. Toss with remaining ingredients in large bowl.

CALIFORNIA BLACK BEAN SALAD

The spicy dressing will make this salad one of your favorites.

1 can (15 ounces) black beans,
   drained and rinsed
1 can (12 ounces) whole kernel
   corn, drained
1 medium tomato, chopped
½ cup chopped red onion

½ cup chopped green bell pepper
½ teaspoon Lawry's Garlic Powder
   with Parsley
Spicy Mexican Dressing (recipe
   follows)

In large bowl, combine all ingredients; blend well. Cover and refrigerate at least
15 minutes. *Makes 6 servings*

PRESENTATION: Garnish with green onion top and red onion slices. Serve
with your favorite Mexican recipes or as a spicy side dish salad.

(Continued)

SPICY MEXICAN DRESSING

¾ cup Italian salad dressing
2 teaspoons chopped cilantro or
parsley
¾ teaspoon hot pepper sauce

½ teaspoon Lawry's Seasoned
Pepper
½ teaspoon chili powder

In small bowl, combine all ingredients; blend well. Cover and refrigerate until
ready to use.   *Makes ¾ cup*

FETTUCCINE SALAD

Lime juice and Dijon mustard give this salad some real zing!

½ cup olive or vegetable oil
⅓ cup grated Parmesan cheese
¼ cup lime juice
5 teaspoons Dijon mustard
¾ teaspoon Lawry's Seasoned
Pepper
¾ teaspoon dried basil, crushed
½ teaspoon Lawry's Seasoned Salt

½ teaspoon Lawry's Garlic Powder
with Parsley
8 ounces fettuccine, cooked and
drained
1 medium tomato, chopped
1 can (2.2 ounces) sliced pitted ripe
olives, drained
1 medium zucchini, sliced

In small bowl, combine oil, Parmesan cheese, lime juice, mustard and seasonings; blend well. In large bowl, combine remaining ingredients. Pour dressing
mixture over fettuccine mixture; toss to coat well. Cover and refrigerate before
serving.   *Makes 4 servings*

PRESENTATION: Sprinkle with additional grated Parmesan cheese.

FRESH AND CREAMY RICE SALAD

A family favorite.

3 cups cooked rice, cooled
1 cucumber, peeled and diced
1 cup (4 ounces) sharp Cheddar
cheese, cut into cubes
¼ cup sliced green onions
½ cup dairy sour cream
1 tablespoon mayonnaise

2 teaspoons lemon juice
1 teaspoon Lawry's Lemon Pepper
Seasoning
1 teaspoon Lawry's Seasoned Salt
8 ounces cooked ham, cut into
2-inch julienne strips

In large bowl, combine all ingredients except ham; blend well. Gently stir in
ham. Cover and refrigerate.   *Makes 6 servings*

PRESENTATION: Garnish with tomato wedges. Serve on bed of shredded
lettuce.

HINT: Cooked, cubed turkey or chicken can be substituted for ham.

MARINATED VEGETABLE SALAD▶

Most of the preparation for this colorful salad can be done well in advance.

8 cherry tomatoes, halved
1 medium carrot, thinly sliced
1 medium zucchini, thinly sliced
1 small onion, sliced and separated
 into rings
½ cup white wine vinegar
¼ cup vegetable oil
¼ cup sugar
¾ teaspoon Lawry's Seasoned Salt
½ to ¾ teaspoon Lawry's Seasoned
 Pepper
½ teaspoon dry mustard
Lettuce leaves
1 package (6 ounces) frozen
 Chinese pea pods, thawed and
 drained

In 10×6×2-inch baking dish, place tomatoes, carrot, zucchini and onion. In small jar with tight-fitting lid, combine vinegar, oil, sugar, Seasoned Salt, Seasoned Pepper and mustard; shake to blend well. Pour over vegetables; marinate 1 hour or cover and refrigerate overnight. Arrange lettuce on platter; arrange marinated vegetables and pea pods around lettuce.

Makes 4 to 6 servings

PRESENTATION: Serve with broiled beef or poultry.

TUNA & WHITE BEAN SALAD

A light and healthful meal.

1 can (16 ounces) white beans
¼ cup olive or vegetable oil
1 tablespoon lemon juice
½ teaspoon Lawry's Seasoned Salt
½ teaspoon Lawry's Seasoned
 Pepper
¼ cup sliced green onions with tops
1 medium tomato, cut into wedges
Lettuce leaves
1 can (6½ ounces) water-packed
 white tuna, drained

Drain beans; rinse under cold running water; spread on paper towels to dry. In small bowl, combine oil, lemon juice, Seasoned Salt and Seasoned Pepper. Place beans in medium bowl; pour dressing over beans. Add green onions and tomato; mix gently. Transfer bean mixture to platter lined with lettuce leaves. Break tuna into chunks and arrange on top.

Makes 4 to 6 servings

PRESENTATION: Serve alone or as part of an antipasto course. Garnish with lemon wedges.

HINT: 1 can (16 ounces) garbanzo beans can be substituted for white beans.

TOMATO-VERMICELLI CUPS

These one-of-a-kind cups are ready in a snap.

6 firm, ripe medium tomatoes
6 ounces vermicelli, cooked and
   drained
1 tablespoon olive or vegetable oil
1½ tablespoons lemon juice
¼ cup plain nonfat yogurt

¼ cup mayonnaise
2 teaspoons snipped fresh chives
1 teaspoon Lawry's Lemon Pepper
   Seasoning
1 teaspoon Lawry's Seasoned Salt

Cut stem ends from tomatoes; carefully remove seeds and pulp. Invert shells on paper towels to drain. Toss pasta with oil and lemon juice; let cool. Add yogurt, mayonnaise, chives, Lemon Pepper Seasoning and Seasoned Salt to pasta; toss gently. Spoon pasta into tomato shells. *Makes 6 servings*

PRESENTATION: Garnish with parsley. Serve with broiled steak or casserole dishes.

HINT: Tomato pulp can be frozen and used later in a sauce, dressing or relish.

TANGY HAWAIIAN DRESSING

A slightly sweet, yet tangy dressing

¼ cup honey
3 tablespoons red wine vinegar
3 tablespoons lemon juice
3 tablespoons water
2 tablespoons pineapple juice

¼ teaspoon Lawry's Seasoned Salt
¼ teaspoon Lawry's Garlic Powder
   with Parsley
⅓ cup vegetable oil

In small jar with tight-fitting lid, combine all ingredients except oil; shake to blend well. Add oil; shake again. Refrigerate several hours or overnight.

Makes about 1 cup

PRESENTATION: Serve with turkey or chicken salads, mixed green salads or a combination of greens and fruit.

HINT: For a creamy dressing, add 1 to 2 tablespoons mayonnaise or dairy sour cream.

MARINATED DANISH CUCUMBERS

An all-time favorite.

3 cucumbers, peeled and thinly
   sliced
1 tablespoon Lawry's Seasoned
   Salt
½ cup white wine vinegar

¼ cup water
1 tablespoon sugar
¾ teaspoon dill weed
½ teaspoon Lawry's Seasoned
   Pepper

In large bowl, combine cucumbers and Seasoned Salt; blend well. Cover and refrigerate 2 hours; drain thoroughly. In small jar with tight-fitting lid, combine remaining ingredients; shake to blend well. Pour over cucumbers; cover and refrigerate several hours or overnight. *Makes 6 servings*

PRESENTATION: Serve ice cold with barbecued foods or picnic basket specialties.

LITE DRESSING

A delicate dressing with just a bite of Lemon Pepper.

¼ cup dry white wine
¼ cup lemon or lime juice
¼ cup vegetable oil

2 teaspoons sugar
2 teaspoons Lawry's Lemon Pepper
   Seasoning

In small jar with tight-fitting lid, combine all ingredients; shake to blend well.

Makes 4 servings

PRESENTATION: Toss with any combination of garden greens.

ISLANDER TURKEY SALAD

A light and refreshing combination.

¼ cup orange juice
3 tablespoons vegetable oil
3 tablespoons red wine vinegar
½ teaspoon Lawry's Garlic Powder
  with Parsley
½ teaspoon grated orange peel
1 large orange, peeled and sliced
  crosswise

1 small cucumber, peeled and sliced
½ small red onion, chopped
  Shredded lettuce
1 can (5 ounces) chunk white
  turkey, drained

In small jar with tight-fitting lid, combine orange juice, oil, vinegar, Garlic Powder with Parsley and orange peel; shake to blend well. In large bowl, combine orange, cucumber and onion with dressing; blend well. Mound orange mixture on shredded lettuce; top with turkey pieces.   *Makes 2 servings*

PRESENTATION: Serve with herbal tea garnished with a mint sprig.

SOUPS

HEARTY VEGETABLE STEW ▶

This home-style stew is ideal to store in the freezer in single-serving portions.

1 can (28 ounces) whole tomatoes,
  cut up
1½ cups water
1 package (1.5 ounces) Lawry's
  Spaghetti Sauce Seasoning
  Blend with Imported
  Mushrooms
1 medium potato, chopped

1 medium onion, chopped
1 package (10 ounces) frozen mixed
  vegetables
1 can (8¾ ounces) garbanzo beans,
  drained
1 teaspoon dried basil, crushed
1 teaspoon Lawry's Garlic Powder
  with Parsley

In Dutch oven, combine tomatoes, water and Spaghetti Sauce Seasoning Blend with Imported Mushrooms; blend well. Add potato and onion. Bring to a boil. Reduce heat; cover and simmer 15 minutes. Add remaining ingredients. Simmer 20 minutes longer.   *Makes 4 to 6 servings*

PRESENTATION: Serve piping hot in bowls; garnish with grated Cheddar cheese and croutons.

HINT: For a one-dish meal, add cooked, shredded chicken or beef stew meat.

BROCCOLI CHEDDAR SOUP

A quick and convenient lunch or light dinner dish.

3 tablespoons butter or margarine
1 small onion, finely chopped
¾ teaspoon Lawry's Seasoned Salt
½ teaspoon Lawry's Garlic Powder
   with Parsley
6 tablespoons all-purpose flour
2 cups milk

1½ cups chicken broth
1 cup beer
1 package (10 ounces) frozen
   chopped broccoli, thawed and
   drained
2½ cups (10 ounces) grated mild
   Cheddar cheese

In Dutch oven, melt butter and sauté onion, Seasoned Salt and Garlic Powder with Parsley until onion is tender. Stir in flour. Gradually whisk in milk. Bring to a boil. Reduce heat; simmer 5 minutes or until thickened. Stir in chicken broth and beer. Return to a boil. Add broccoli; reduce heat and add Cheddar cheese. Stir until cheese is melted.   *Makes 4 to 6 servings*

PRESENTATION: Serve with hearty whole grain bread, rolls or garlic toast.

EASY HOME-STYLE CORN CHOWDER

A full-flavored soup that tastes like it took all day to cook.

2 cans (12 ounces each) whole
   kernel corn, drained
3 tablespoons butter or margarine
1 small onion, chopped
½ cup diced red bell pepper
   (optional)
3 tablespoons all-purpose flour

2 to 2½ cups milk
1 cup half-and-half
1 teaspoon Lawry's Seasoned
   Pepper
½ teaspoon Lawry's Seasoned Salt
⅛ teaspoon ground nutmeg

In food processor or blender, purée corn; set aside. In large saucepan, melt butter and sauté onion and red pepper 5 minutes. Add flour and blend to a smooth paste; remove from heat and whisk in milk and half-and-half. Add puréed corn, Seasoned Pepper, Seasoned Salt and nutmeg. Bring to a boil, stirring constantly, about 5 minutes. Serve hot.   *Makes 4 to 6 servings*

PRESENTATION: Serve with crispy bread sticks or piping hot French bread.

HINT: For a sweeter chowder, 1 can (16 ounces) creamed corn with liquid can be substituted for the whole kernel corn. Substitute water for the half-and-half.

CALIFORNIA CHICKEN SOUP

A wonderfully pleasing homemade soup.

3 cans (14½ ounces each) chicken
  broth
1 cup water
2 cups cooked cubed chicken
1 small onion, chopped
½ cup sliced carrots
1 teaspoon Lawry's Lemon Pepper
  Seasoning
½ to ¾ teaspoon dried oregano,
  crushed

½ teaspoon Lawry's Garlic Powder
  with Parsley
1 bay leaf
4 ounces cheese tortellini or shell
  pasta
1 package (9 ounces) frozen cut
  broccoli, thawed

In Dutch oven, combine all ingredients except tortellini and broccoli. Bring to a boil. Add tortellini. Reduce heat; simmer, uncovered, 25 minutes. Add broccoli; simmer 10 minutes or until broccoli and tortellini are tender. Remove bay leaf. Serve hot.   *Makes 4 to 6 servings*

PRESENTATION: Serve with Cheddar cheese biscuits.

HINT: 1 bag (1 pound) assorted frozen vegetables can be substituted for the onion, carrots and broccoli.

CONDIMENTS

GARLIC MAYONNAISE SAUCE

A versatile sauce.

1 cup mayonnaise
½ cup milk
1 teaspoon Lawry's Garlic Powder
  with Parsley

1 teaspoon lemon juice
½ teaspoon Lawry's Seasoned
  Pepper

In blender or food processor, combine all ingredients; process until well blended. Cover and refrigerate until ready to use.   *Makes 1½ cups*

PRESENTATION: Use as a sandwich spread or as a sauce for vegetables or grilled steak.

HINT: For a low-cal version, use reduced-calorie mayonnaise and skim milk *or* plain nonfat yogurt; omit lemon juice if using yogurt.

CORN 'N' PEPPER RELISH

A new twist on old-fashioned corn relish.

3 tablespoons white wine vinegar
1 tablespoon sugar
½ teaspoon Lawry's Seasoned Salt
⅛ teaspoon hot pepper sauce
  (optional)
⅛ teaspoon mustard seed

1 can (8¾ ounces) whole kernel
  corn, drained
½ cup chopped green bell pepper
¼ cup chopped red bell pepper *or*
  2 tablespoons diced pimiento
1 tablespoon sliced green onion

In small saucepan, combine vinegar, sugar, Seasoned Salt, hot pepper sauce and mustard seed. Bring to a boil. Remove from heat and add remaining ingredients; blend well. Cover and refrigerate overnight to blend flavors.
    Makes 1¾ cups

PRESENTATION: Serve warm with roasted meat or poultry or as a cold salad mixed with chilled rice.

CHUNKY TOMATO RELISH

A zesty accompaniment for grilled poultry and beef.

2 cups chopped tomatoes
3 tablespoons vinegar
3 tablespoons olive or vegetable oil
2 tablespoons chopped onion
2 tablespoons capers, drained and rinsed
2 tablespoons packed brown sugar

1 teaspoon Lawry's Seasoned Salt
1 teaspoon Lawry's Seasoned Pepper
1 teaspoon ground ginger
1 teaspoon mustard seed
½ teaspoon Lawry's Garlic Powder with Parsley

In large, nonstick saucepan, combine all ingredients. Bring to a boil. Reduce heat; simmer, uncovered, 20 minutes, stirring frequently. Pour into medium bowl. Set bowl in larger bowl of ice to stop cooking. Cover and refrigerate.

Makes 1½ cups

PRESENTATION: Serve warm or cold.

CREOLE SAUCE FOR CORN-ON-THE-COB

This is a great sauce for almost any vegetable.

8 ears fresh corn, *unhusked*
¾ cup butter or margarine
¼ cup minced green bell pepper
¼ cup minced red bell pepper
¼ cup minced green onions
2 teaspoons Lawry's Seasoned Salt

1 teaspoon dried thyme, crushed
¼ teaspoon Lawry's Garlic Powder
  with Parsley
1 bay leaf, crumbled
¼ cup dry white wine
1 tablespoon lemon juice

Place corn in large bowl and cover with cold water; let soak overnight. Grill corn in husk over medium-low coals 20 to 25 minutes or until tender. In medium, heavy saucepan, melt butter and sauté green and red peppers, onions, Seasoned Salt, thyme, Garlic Powder with Parsley and bay leaf 1 to 2 minutes. Add wine and lemon juice and cook 2 minutes. Remove bay leaf. Dip corn in sauce or pour sauce over husked corn. *Makes 8 servings*

PRESENTATION: Pull corn husks and silk back to use as "handles."

LEMON-DILL SAUCE

Try this sauce with any number of different vegetables such as broccoli, green beans, cauliflower, peas or zucchini.

½ cup milk
1 package (3 ounces) cream cheese,
  softened
1 tablespoon minced onion
¾ teaspoon Lawry's Lemon Pepper
  Seasoning

½ teaspoon Lawry's Seasoned Salt
½ teaspoon dill weed
½ teaspoon lemon juice

In small saucepan, combine all ingredients. Heat just to boiling, stirring constantly, until smooth. Add extra milk to thin, if necessary.

Makes 4 servings

PRESENTATION: Pour over vegetables, or use as a sauce for grilled or poached fish.

POTATOES & RICE

DELUXE POTATO BAKE

A satisfying potato casserole to serve to family and friends.

2 eggs, beaten
¼ cup unseasoned dry bread crumbs
2 green onions with tops, chopped
2 tablespoons milk
¾ teaspoon Lawry's Seasoned
    Pepper
½ teaspoon Lawry's Seasoned Salt

2 large potatoes, peeled, grated and
    held in ice water
1 cup (4 ounces) grated Cheddar
    cheese
4 bacon slices, cooked and
    crumbled

In large bowl, combine eggs, bread crumbs, onions, milk, Seasoned Pepper and
Seasoned Salt. Drain potatoes and stir into egg mixture. Add ½ of Cheddar
cheese and ½ of bacon. Spoon mixture into lightly greased 8×8×2-inch casserole. Bake, uncovered, in 350°F oven 20 minutes. Sprinkle with remaining
cheese and bacon; bake 5 minutes longer.   *Makes 4 servings*

PRESENTATION: Garnish with additional cooked bacon and parsley. Serve
with grilled hamburgers or steak instead of french fries.

HINT: For quicker preparation, use unpeeled potatoes.

FRUITED RICE PILAF ▶

Dried fruits are the key to this delicious and unusual recipe.

2½ cups water
1 cup rice
2 tablespoons butter or margarine
1 medium tomato, chopped
⅓ cup minced dried apples
¼ cup minced dried apricots

¼ cup sliced green onions
¾ teaspoon Lawry's Seasoned Salt
¼ teaspoon Lawry's Garlic Powder
  with Parsley
3 tablespoons sliced almonds

In 2-quart saucepan, bring water to a boil; add rice and butter. Return to a boil. Reduce heat; cover and simmer 15 minutes. Add remaining ingredients except almonds and cook 5 to 10 minutes longer or until rice is tender. Stir in almonds.   *Makes 4 servings*

PRESENTATION: Garnish with apple slices and celery leaves. Serve with baked pork chops, roasted meats or poultry.

HINT: For variety and added flavor, try adding ¼ teaspoon curry powder to cooked rice.

MASHED POTATOES PLUS

Cream cheese is the "plus" in this quick side dish.

1⅔ cups water
1⅓ cups potato buds
1 package (3 ounces) cream cheese,
  cubed

½ to 1 teaspoon Lawry's Seasoned
  Salt

In medium saucepan, bring water to a boil. Add potatoes, cream cheese and Seasoned Salt; blend well.   *Makes 4 servings*

PRESENTATION: Garnish with chopped parsley. Serve with meat loaf, fried chicken or any hearty entrée.

TACO TOTS

Super easy spicy potato bites.

1 package (32 ounces) frozen tater
  tots

1 package (1.25 ounces) Lawry's
  Taco Seasoning Mix

In large plastic bag, combine tater tots and Taco Seasoning Mix. Seal bag and shake to coat potatoes with seasoning. Spread tater tots on foil-covered cookie sheet. Bake in 450°F oven 15 to 20 minutes or until crisp.
                                      Makes 8 to 10 servings

PRESENTATION: Serve with mixture of ½ ketchup and ½ mild salsa.

ORANGE WILD RICE

A tempting side dish perfect for family or company.

1 medium orange
Chicken broth
2 tablespoons butter or margarine
¾ cup wild rice, rinsed well
1 small onion, chopped
½ teaspoon Lawry's Seasoned Pepper

¼ teaspoon Lawry's Garlic Powder with Parsley
1 package (10 ounces) frozen peas, thawed
⅓ cup chopped pecans

Grate peel from orange; set aside. Squeeze juice from orange; add enough chicken broth to juice to measure 1¼ cups. In large saucepan, melt butter and sauté rice and onion, stirring frequently. Add orange juice mixture, orange peel, Seasoned Pepper and Garlic Powder with Parsley. Bring to a boil. Reduce heat; cover and simmer 35 minutes or until liquid is absorbed. Stir in peas and pecans; simmer 3 to 5 minutes longer or until peas are tender.

Makes 4 to 6 servings

PRESENTATION: Garnish with Mandarin orange segments. Serve with roast pork.

PATRICK'S OVEN POTATOES

A wonderfully easy side dish.

**4 to 5 medium russet potatoes,
scrubbed and cut into ½-inch
cubes**
1 small onion, thinly sliced
**¾ teaspoon Lawry's Seasoned
Pepper**

¾ teaspoon Lawry's Seasoned Salt
**½ teaspoon Lawry's Garlic Powder
with Parsley**
⅓ cup vegetable oil

In large bowl, toss potatoes and onion with seasonings to coat well. Pour mixture into 1½-quart baking dish. Drizzle with oil. Cover with aluminum foil and bake in 375°F oven 35 to 40 minutes or until potatoes are tender.

Makes 4 to 6 servings

PRESENTATION: Sprinkle with chopped parsley. Serve with steak or roast chicken.

MICROWAVE DIRECTIONS: Pour potato mixture into microwave-safe 1½-quart baking dish; drizzle with oil. Cover with vented plastic wrap and microwave on HIGH 10 to 15 minutes or until tender, stirring after 5 minutes. Drain on paper towels.

PARMESAN POTATOES ▶

A perfect side dish to almost any main dish.

2 tablespoons butter or margarine
2 medium russet potatoes, peeled
  and sliced ¼ inch thick
⅓ cup chopped onion
½ teaspoon Lawry's Seasoned Salt

½ teaspoon Lawry's Garlic Salt
½ teaspoon Lawry's Seasoned
  Pepper
½ cup grated Parmesan cheese
⅓ cup chopped green bell pepper

MICROWAVE DIRECTIONS: In microwave-safe baking dish, place butter. Microwave on HIGH 30 seconds or until melted. In large bowl, combine potatoes, onion and seasonings; blend well. Transfer to baking dish; cover with vented plastic wrap. Microwave on HIGH 10 minutes, stirring after 5 minutes. Mix in Parmesan cheese and green pepper. Microwave, uncovered, on HIGH 5 minutes. Let stand 2 minutes before serving.   *Makes 4 servings*

PRESENTATION: Sprinkle with minced parsley.

CHEDDAR CHEESY RICE

A touch of onion and cheese highlight this rice dish.

2 tablespoons butter or margarine
⅓ cup chopped onion
2 cups water
1 cup rice
1 cup (4 ounces) grated Cheddar
  cheese

2 tablespoons grated Parmesan
  cheese
2 tablespoons chopped parsley
1 teaspoon Lawry's Garlic Powder
  with Parsley
¾ teaspoon Lawry's Seasoned Salt

In medium saucepan, melt butter and sauté onion. Add water and rice. Bring to a boil. Reduce heat; cover and simmer 20 minutes or until rice is tender. Add remaining ingredients; blend well and serve immediately.
          Makes 4 to 6 servings

PRESENTATION: Serve as a side dish with hamburgers or chicken recipes.

VEGETABLES

SNAPPY PODS AMANDINE ▶

An exciting Oriental dish to add to your meal.

½ cup cold water
1 tablespoon soy sauce
2 teaspoons cornstarch
1 teaspoon instant chicken bouillon
  granules
½ teaspoon Lawry's Seasoned
  Pepper

½ teaspoon Lawry's Garlic Salt
1 tablespoon vegetable oil
1 package (6 ounces) frozen
  Chinese pea pods, thawed
½ cup sliced fresh mushrooms
2 tablespoons toasted, slivered
  almonds

In small bowl, combine water, soy sauce, cornstarch, bouillon granules, Seasoned Pepper and Garlic Salt; blend well and set aside. In large skillet, heat oil and stir-fry pea pods 2 minutes. Stir in mushrooms. Add cornstarch mixture; cook and stir until thickened and glazed. Sprinkle with almonds.

Makes 4 servings

PRESENTATION: Serve with other Chinese dishes or grilled steak or fish.

HINT: 1 can (4 ounces) sliced mushrooms, drained, can be substituted for the fresh mushrooms.

ZUCCHINI MEXICANA

Versatile zucchini with just a hint of Mexican seasoning.

2 tablespoons vegetable oil
1 onion, thinly sliced
1½ pounds zucchini, thinly sliced
1 can (14½ ounces) whole
  tomatoes, drained (reserving
  ¼ cup juice)

1 can (4 ounces) diced green chiles
1 teaspoon Lawry's Seasoned Salt
¾ teaspoon Lawry's Garlic Powder
  with Parsley
1 cup (4 ounces) grated Monterey
  Jack cheese

In medium skillet, heat oil and sauté onion until tender; add remaining ingredients except Monterey Jack cheese. Bring to a boil. Reduce heat; simmer, uncovered, 5 to 10 minutes or until zucchini is tender. Place zucchini mixture in 8×8×2-inch baking dish; top with cheese. Bake, uncovered, in 375°F oven 10 minutes or until cheese melts.

Makes 6 to 8 servings

PRESENTATION: Serve with other Mexican specialties.

SOUTHERN-STYLE GLAZED CARROTS

Get your kids interested in vegetables with this sweet and crunchy side dish.

1 pound carrots, cut into ¼-inch
    slices *or* 1 pound frozen sliced
    carrots
½ cup pineapple juice
¼ cup packed brown sugar
2 tablespoons butter or margarine

¾ teaspoon cornstarch
½ teaspoon Lawry's Seasoned Salt
½ teaspoon ground cinnamon
¼ teaspoon ground allspice
¼ cup chopped pecans or walnuts

In large saucepan, cook carrots in boiling water to cover until tender. Drain and set aside. In same saucepan, combine remaining ingredients except pecans. Bring to a boil. Reduce heat; simmer, uncovered, 5 minutes. Add carrots and pecans; toss to coat with glaze mixture.   *Makes 4 to 6 servings*

PRESENTATION: Garnish with fresh cilantro or parsley. Serve as a side dish with fried chicken or roasted meats.

VEGETABLES ROMA

An Italian vegetable combination in a savory spaghetti sauce.

1 package (1.5 ounces) Lawry's
    Extra Rich & Thick Spaghetti
    Sauce Seasoning Blend
1 can (6 ounces) tomato paste
1¾ cups water
2 tablespoons butter or vegetable
    oil
1 small eggplant, peeled and cubed

1 package (10 ounces) frozen
    Italian green beans, thawed
¼ pound fresh mushrooms, sliced
½ cup (2 ounces) grated mozzarella
    cheese
2 tablespoons grated Parmesan
    cheese

In medium saucepan, prepare Extra Rich & Thick Spaghetti Sauce Seasoning Blend according to package directions using tomato paste, water and butter. Add eggplant, green beans and mushrooms. Return to a boil. Reduce heat; simmer, uncovered, 25 minutes. Transfer to serving dish and top with mozzarella and Parmesan cheeses. *Makes 6 servings*

PRESENTATION: Serve with any of your favorite main dishes.

HINT: For variety, try substituting 1 package (10 ounces) frozen artichoke hearts for the eggplant.

GREEN BEANS WITH TOMATO DRESSING

Spice up steamed green beans with this fragrant tomato-tarragon sauce.

1 pound fresh green beans, stems
    and strings removed
1 tablespoon butter or margarine
1 cup chopped onion
1 can (14½ ounces) whole
    tomatoes, cut up

1 tablespoon white wine vinegar
1 tablespoon chopped parsley
½ teaspoon dried tarragon, crushed
½ teaspoon Lawry's Seasoned Salt
¼ teaspoon Lawry's Garlic Powder
    with Parsley

Cut beans in half. In medium saucepan with steamer insert, steam beans over boiling water 15 minutes or until tender-crisp. Drain; set aside. In medium skillet, melt butter and sauté onion 5 minutes. Stir in remaining ingredients. Bring to a boil. Reduce heat; simmer, uncovered, 10 minutes. Arrange beans on platter; spoon warm sauce over beans. *Makes 4 to 6 servings*

PRESENTATION: Serve with fish fillets and whipped potatoes.

GRILLED VEGETABLE KABOBS ▶

A simple way to serve vegetables.

½ cup vegetable oil
⅓ cup lemon juice
3 tablespoons red wine
1 tablespoon Lawry's Lemon
  Pepper Seasoning
2 teaspoons red pepper flakes
1 teaspoon Lawry's Seasoned Salt
1 yellow crookneck squash, cut into
  chunks

1 medium zucchini, cut into chunks
1 small onion, cut into wedges
16 medium mushroom caps
  Cherry tomatoes
3 tablespoons grated Parmesan
  cheese

In large bowl, combine oil, lemon juice, wine, Lemon Pepper Seasoning, red pepper flakes and Seasoned Salt; blend well. Add vegetables; cover and refrigerate 30 minutes or overnight. Remove vegetables; reserve marinade. Thread vegetables onto metal or wooden skewers. (If using wooden skewers, soak them in water 15 to 20 minutes before adding vegetables.) Broil kabobs 6 inches from heat 12 to 15 minutes, brushing often with reserved marinade. Sprinkle with Parmesan cheese and broil until lightly browned.

Makes 4 to 6 servings

PRESENTATION: Serve over steamed rice. Serve with oven-baked chicken.

HINT: For a main dish, add chicken or beef cubes to skewers before broiling.

EASY BROCCOLI SOUFFLÉ

The easiest soufflé recipe, ever!

1½ cups cooked broccoli, thoroughly
  drained
1½ cups milk
4 eggs

½ cup (2 ounces) grated Cheddar
  cheese
¾ teaspoon Lawry's Seasoned Salt

In blender or food processor, purée broccoli. Add remaining ingredients; blend well. Pour into medium casserole; bake, uncovered, in 400°F oven 20 minutes, or until soufflé is puffy and top is browned. Serve immediately.

Makes 6 servings

PRESENTATION: Sprinkle with additional grated Cheddar cheese.

HINT: Other vegetables, such as carrots or peas, can be substituted for the broccoli.

LAYERED HERBED TOMATOES

Using the microwave oven makes this a quicker-than-quick side dish.

1 package (6 ounces) seasoned
   croutons
⅓ cup vegetable oil
3 tablespoons red wine vinegar
6 tomatoes, cut into ½-inch slices
6 ounces Monterey Jack or
   mozzarella cheese, thinly sliced

2 tablespoons dried basil, crushed
1 tablespoon snipped fresh chives
½ teaspoon Lawry's Seasoned Salt
½ teaspoon Lawry's Seasoned
   Pepper

MICROWAVE DIRECTIONS: In bottom of microwave-safe baking dish, sprinkle croutons. In small bowl, combine oil and vinegar. Pour ⅓ of oil mixture over croutons. Layer slices of tomato and Monterey Jack cheese over croutons, overlapping to fit. Sprinkle with basil, chives, Seasoned Salt and Seasoned Pepper. Microwave on HIGH 5 to 7 minutes. Spoon remaining oil mixture over tomatoes. Let stand, covered, 5 minutes before serving.

Makes 4 to 6 servings

PRESENTATION: Serve with grilled chicken breasts and steamed green beans.

SUMMER SQUASH SAUTÉ

An appealing, colorful side dish.

1 tablespoon butter or margarine
1 small red bell pepper, cut into
   strips
2 small yellow crookneck squash,
   cut into ¼-inch diagonal slices
2 small zucchini, sliced

½ medium onion, sliced
1 cup cherry tomato halves
1½ teaspoons Lawry's Lemon Pepper
   Seasoning
½ teaspoon Lawry's Garlic Salt
¼ teaspoon dried oregano, crushed

In large skillet, melt butter and sauté red pepper, crookneck squash and zucchini 5 minutes. Stir in onion, tomatoes, Lemon Pepper Seasoning, Garlic Salt and oregano. Cover and cook over low heat 5 to 10 minutes or until tender.

Makes 4 to 6 servings

PRESENTATION: Serve with fresh fish steaks or turkey cutlets.

HINT: Place final mixture in casserole, top with ½ cup (4 ounces) grated Cheddar cheese. Place under broiler 2 minutes or until cheese is lightly browned.

LITE AND LEMONY CAULIFLOWER

Add a tangy touch to cauliflower with this easy-to-make sauce.

1 head cauliflower, cored and leaves
   removed
½ cup plain nonfat yogurt
¼ cup mayonnaise

2 tablespoons sliced green onion
2 teaspoons Dijon mustard
2 teaspoons Lawry's Lemon Pepper
   Seasoning

In Dutch oven, cook cauliflower in boiling water 20 minutes or until tender. Drain and cut into bite-size pieces. In small bowl, combine remaining ingredients; pour over cauliflower.

Makes 4 to 6 servings

PRESENTATION: Serve with hearty beef and roast chicken entrées.

MICROWAVE DIRECTIONS: Place cauliflower in microwave-safe pie plate with 1 cup water. Cover with vented plastic wrap and microwave on HIGH 6 to 10 minutes or until tender. Drain.

CREAMED SPINACH À LA LAWRY'S ▶

This famous recipe is served at Lawry's The Prime Rib restaurants in Beverly Hills, Chicago and Dallas.

4 bacon slices, finely chopped
1 cup finely chopped onion
¼ cup all-purpose flour
2 teaspoons Lawry's Seasoned Salt
½ teaspoon Lawry's Seasoned Pepper

½ teaspoon Lawry's Garlic Powder with Parsley
1½ to 2 cups milk
2 packages (10 ounces each) frozen spinach, cooked and drained

In medium skillet, cook bacon until almost crisp. Add onion to bacon and cook until onion is tender, about 10 minutes. Remove from heat. Add flour, Seasoned Salt, Seasoned Pepper and Garlic Powder with Parsley; blend well. Gradually stir in milk, starting with 1½ cups; cook and stir over low heat until thickened. Add spinach and mix thoroughly. If too thick, add additional milk.

Makes 8 servings

PRESENTATION: Garnish with fresh basil and additional cooked bacon. Excellent with prime ribs of beef.

BROCCOLI CONCERTO

This colorful side dish is a breeze to make in the microwave oven.

Juice of 1 medium orange
2 tablespoons olive or vegetable oil
2 tablespoons red wine vinegar
2 tablespoons cornstarch
1 tablespoon Dijon mustard

½ teaspoon Lawry's Lemon Pepper Seasoning
¼ teaspoon sugar
2 cups broccoli flowerettes
2 red bell peppers, cut into chunks

MICROWAVE DIRECTIONS: In medium, microwave-safe bowl, whisk together all ingredients except broccoli and red peppers. Microwave on HIGH 3 minutes, stirring often. In separate larger microwave-safe bowl, combine broccoli and red pepper; cover with vented plastic wrap and microwave on HIGH 5 minutes until tender. Drain. Pour hot dressing over vegetables and toss to coat well.

Makes 4 servings

PRESENTATION: Serve with fresh fish fillets and brown rice.

BREADS

CRISPIE CHEESE TWISTS ▶

Add a "twist" to hearty soups or fresh salad. They make a great appetizer, as well.

½ cup grated Parmesan cheese
¾ teaspoon Lawry's Seasoned
   Pepper
½ teaspoon Lawry's Garlic Powder
   with Parsley

1 package (17¼ ounces) frozen puff
   pastry, thawed
1 egg white, lightly beaten

In small bowl, combine Parmesan cheese, Seasoned Pepper and Garlic Powder with Parsley. Unfold pastry sheets onto cutting board. Brush pastry lightly with egg white; sprinkle each sheet with ¼ of the cheese mixture. Lightly press into pastry; turn over and repeat. Cut each sheet into 12 (1-inch-wide) strips; twist. Place on .greased cookie sheet and bake in 350°F oven 15 minutes or until golden brown.   *Makes 2 dozen*

PRESENTATION: Serve in a napkin-lined basket. Place layer of plastic wrap over napkin to protect napkin.

HINT: To make 1 dozen, use only one of the two packaged pastry sheets; reduce cheese and seasonings by half.

MILANO-STYLE DINNER ROLLS

A creamy cheese topping adds delicious flavor and texture to dinner rolls.

1 cup ricotta cheese
¼ cup grated Parmesan cheese
2 tablespoons chopped green onion
¾ teaspoon Lawry's Garlic Powder
   with Parsley

6 to 8 small Italian dinner rolls,
   sliced lengthwise

In small bowl, combine ricotta cheese, Parmesan cheese, green onion and Garlic Powder with Parsley; blend well. Spread cheese mixture on each half dinner roll. Broil under medium heat until cheese is lightly browned.
              Makes 6 to 8 servings

PRESENTATION: Serve warm as an accompaniment to Italian dishes.

FIESTA CORN BREAD

A colorful and spicy version of a favorite bread.

1 box (15 ounces) corn bread mix
1 can (8¾ ounces) whole kernel
   corn, drained
1 cup milk
1 can (4 ounces) diced green chiles

1 jar (2 ounces) diced pimientos,
   drained
1 egg, beaten
1 teaspoon Lawry's Seasoned Salt

In large bowl, combine all ingredients; blend well. Pour into greased 8×8×2-inch baking dish. Bake, uncovered, in 425°F oven 25 to 30 minutes or until toothpick inserted in center comes out clean. *Makes 6 to 8 servings*

PRESENTATION: Serve warm with butter.

DENVER ONION-BEER MUFFINS

A hearty addition to your menu.

3 cups self-rising flour
2 tablespoons sugar
1 teaspoon dried basil, crushed
½ teaspoon Lawry's Seasoned
  Pepper
½ teaspoon Lawry's Garlic Powder
  with Parsley

1 can (12 ounces) beer
1 small onion, finely chopped
1 tablespoon butter or margarine,
  melted
1 egg beaten with 1 tablespoon
  water

In large bowl, combine flour, sugar, basil, Seasoned Pepper and Garlic Powder with Parsley. Stir in beer, onion and butter just until blended; dough will be sticky. Fill greased 2½-inch muffin cups ⅔ full. Brush with egg mixture; let stand 10 minutes. Bake in 350°F oven on bottom shelf 25 minutes or until toothpick inserted in center comes out clean. Cool on wire rack 5 minutes. Remove from muffin cups.   *Makes 1½ dozen*

PRESENTATION: Serve warm with whipped butter or sprinkle shredded Cheddar cheese over broken muffins and place under broiler 1 minute.

BISCUIT BREAD ITALIANO

Quickly blend the ingredients together and let bake while you do something else.

1½ cups buttermilk
1 egg, beaten
3 cups biscuit mix
1 cup (4 ounces) shredded Cheddar
  cheese
1 can (2.2 ounces) sliced pitted ripe
  olives, drained

1 package (1.5 ounces) Lawry's
  Spaghetti Sauce Seasoning
  Blend with Imported
  Mushrooms

In large bowl, combine buttermilk and egg. Stir in remaining ingredients; blend well. Spoon batter into greased 9×5×3-inch loaf pan. Bake in 350°F oven 45 to 50 minutes or until toothpick inserted into center comes out clean. Turn out on wire rack to cool.   *Makes 12 servings*

PRESENTATION: Serve with soups and salads.

HINTS: For a hearty bread, add 1½ cups chopped salami or pepperoni to dough. For drop biscuits, do not pour batter into loaf pan; drop batter by large spoonfuls onto greased baking sheet. Bake 30 minutes or until toothpick inserted into center comes out clean.

WEEKDAY ENTERTAINING

Here are five complete meals for "special" home occasions: Sports Night, Dad's Night to Cook, Casual or Elegant Entertaining and Backyard Family Dinner. Whether you're looking for an easy dinner for your family, or for that special something to offer guests, you're sure to find great serving ideas here.

MONDAY
Sports Night

TURKEY TACO TAMPICO

Unconventional tacos for easy entertaining.

1 package (1.25 ounces) Lawry's Taco Seasoning Mix	2 cups (8 ounces) grated Cheddar or Monterey Jack cheese
1 pound ground turkey	¾ cup chopped red onion
¾ cup water	2 medium tomatoes, chopped
8 flour tortillas	1 medium zucchini, coarsely grated
2 cups shredded lettuce	1 avocado, cubed

In large skillet, prepare Taco Seasoning Mix with ground turkey and water according to package directions. Wrap flour tortillas in aluminum foil and place in 325°F oven 10 minutes to warm. Top each tortilla with ¼ cup of the prepared turkey mixture, lettuce, Cheddar cheese, onion, tomatoes, zucchini and avocado. *Makes 4 to 8 servings*

PRESENTATION: Garnish each taco with dairy sour cream, salsa or Thousand Island Dressing.

Clockwise from top left: Chicken Enchilada Casserole (page 78), Mexican Fudge Sauce (page 79), Guacamole Enchantro (page 78), Tangy Orange Vinaigrette (page 79) and Turkey Taco Tampico.

CHICKEN ENCHILADA CASSEROLE

For a crowd-pleasing entrée, just double the recipe.

2 tablespoons vegetable oil
1 medium onion, chopped
4 cups cooked shredded chicken or turkey
1 can (15 ounces) tomato sauce
1 can (14½ ounces) whole tomatoes, cut up
1 package (1.25 ounces) Lawry's Taco Seasoning Mix
½ teaspoon Lawry's Garlic Powder with Parsley
1 dozen corn tortillas
3 cups (12 ounces) grated Monterey Jack cheese
2 cans (2.2 ounces each) sliced pitted ripe olives

In large skillet, heat oil and sauté onion. Add chicken, tomato sauce, tomatoes, Taco Seasoning Mix and Garlic Powder with Parsley; blend well. Bring to a boil. Reduce heat; simmer, uncovered, 15 minutes. Place 4 corn tortillas in 13×9×2-inch baking dish. Pour ⅓ of chicken mixture on tortillas, spreading evenly. Layer ⅓ of Monterey Jack cheese and ⅓ of olives on top of chicken mixture. Repeat layers 2 times, ending with olives. Bake, uncovered, in 350°F oven 30 to 40 minutes or until cheese is bubbly and casserole is heated through. *Makes 6 to 8 servings*

PRESENTATION: Serve with Mexican rice and green salad.

GUACAMOLE ENCHANTRO

A must to round out hearty Mexican meals.

2 medium avocados, coarsely mashed
1 medium tomato, chopped
½ cup chopped onion
1 tablespoon chopped cilantro or parsley
1 teaspoon Lawry's Garlic Powder with Parsley
¾ teaspoon Lawry's Seasoned Salt

In medium bowl, combine all ingredients; blend well. Cover and refrigerate until ready to serve. *Makes about 2 cups*

PRESENTATION: Garnish with fresh cilantro or parsley. Serve with tortilla chips as an appetizer or snack. Also an ideal topping for classic Mexican recipes.

HINT: To prevent guacamole from turning brown, place plastic wrap directly on the surface of guacamole.

TANGY ORANGE VINAIGRETTE

Orange juice gives this dressing its wonderful flavor.

½ cup vegetable oil
3 tablespoons orange juice
3 tablespoons white wine vinegar
1 tablespoon sliced almonds
1 tablespoon chopped pimiento

¾ teaspoon chopped cilantro or parsley
½ teaspoon Lawry's Seasoned Salt
¼ teaspoon Lawry's Seasoned Pepper

In small jar with tight-fitting lid, combine all ingredients; shake to blend well. Refrigerate until ready to serve. *Makes about 1 cup*

PRESENTATION: Serve on a red onion, orange and lettuce salad.

MEXICAN FUDGE SAUCE

A classic Mexican topping with a hint of cinnamon.

1 cup chocolate fudge ice cream topping

1 tablespoon vanilla extract
1 teaspoon ground cinnamon

In top of double boiler over simmering water, combine all ingredients; blend well. Heat 5 minutes or until warm. *Makes 1 cup*

PRESENTATION: Serve over vanilla ice cream, angel food cake or brownies.

TUESDAY
Dad's Night to Cook

COLESLAW SUPREME

A touch of sweetness and zing!

4 cups shredded green cabbage
2 cups shredded red cabbage
1 can (8 ounces) peaches, drained and cubed
½ cup chopped celery

⅓ cup chopped green onions
¼ cup chopped dry roasted peanuts
¼ cup French salad dressing
½ teaspoon Lawry's Garlic Salt
¼ teaspoon celery seed

In large bowl, combine all ingredients; blend well. Cover and refrigerate at least 30 minutes to blend flavors. *Makes 4 to 6 servings*

PRESENTATION: Serve with sandwiches or barbecued foods.

POCKET FULL OF CHICKEN

*Prepare ahead of time and then reheat in the microwave,
conventional or toaster oven.*

2 cans (5 ounces each) white meat
  chicken, drained
¾ cup (3 ounces) cubed Cheddar
  cheese
½ cup sliced celery
1 medium carrot, grated
3 tablespoons raisins

⅓ cup mayonnaise
½ teaspoon Lawry's Seasoned Salt
¼ teaspoon Lawry's Seasoned
  Pepper
1 roll (9.5 ounces) deli pastry dough
  pockets

In medium bowl, flake chicken. Add remaining ingredients except pastry dough
pockets; blend well. Unroll pastry dough pockets and place ½ cup filling on
each dough pocket. Fold to form triangles and seal edges. Place dough triangles
on cookie sheet. Bake in 375°F oven 12 to 17 minutes or until golden brown
and flaky.   *Makes 4 servings*

PRESENTATION: Serve with Coleslaw Supreme or a hearty soup.

HINT: 1 can (8 ounces) refrigerated quick crescent rolls can be substituted for
the deli pastry pockets.

ROCKY ROAD SQUARES

Easy to prepare and even better to eat!

1 package (12 ounces) semi-sweet
  chocolate chips

1½ cups miniature marshmallows
¾ cup chopped walnuts or pecans

In top of double boiler over simmering water, melt chocolate. Remove from
heat and stir in marshmallows and nuts. Line 8×8×2-inch baking dish with
aluminum foil. Spread chocolate mixture in baking dish; cover and refrigerate
at least 1 hour or until set.   *Makes 16 servings*

PRESENTATION: Cut into 2-inch squares. Wrap leftovers in aluminum foil
and store in refrigerator.

HINT: Milk chocolate chips may be substituted for the semi-sweet chocolate
chips. Or you may use a combination of both.

*On the dinner plate: Coleslaw Supreme (page 79) and
Pocket Full of Chicken. Upper right: Rocky Road Squares.*

WEDNESDAY
Casual Entertaining

FLORENTINE YOGURT DIP

An irresistible dip—and good for you, too.

1 cup chopped fresh spinach
1 cup plain nonfat yogurt
¾ cup reduced-calorie mayonnaise
2 tablespoons lemon juice
1 teaspoon Lawry's Seasoned Salt
½ teaspoon Lawry's Seasoned Pepper
¼ teaspoon Lawry's Garlic Powder with Parsley
¼ teaspoon dried oregano, crushed
¼ teaspoon dried basil, crushed
¼ teaspoon dry mustard

In saucepan with steamer insert, steam spinach over boiling water to wilt. Rinse under cold running water; drain and squeeze out excess moisture. In medium bowl, combine spinach and remaining ingredients; blend well. Cover and refrigerate at least 30 minutes. *Makes about 2 cups*

PRESENTATION: Serve with crisp vegetables or Italian pita sticks.

HINT: 1 (10-ounce) package frozen chopped spinach, thawed and thoroughly drained, can be substituted for the fresh spinach.

ITALIAN PITA STICKS

A simple snack to prepare with leftover pita breads.

¼ cup butter or margarine, softened
1 tablespoon grated Parmesan cheese
¼ teaspoon Lawry's Garlic Powder with Parsley
¼ to ½ teaspoon dried oregano or basil, crushed
2 pita breads, split

In medium bowl, combine butter, Parmesan cheese, Garlic Powder with Parsley and oregano; blend well. Spread mixture on rough side of each pita round; cut into ¼-inch wide strips. Arrange pita strips in a single layer on cookie sheet. Bake in 350°F oven 7 to 9 minutes or until lightly browned. Cool.
Makes 2 dozen

PRESENTATION: Serve with a hearty soup or as an appetizer with prepared Lawry's Spaghetti Sauce Seasoning Blend with Imported Mushrooms.

Clockwise from top left: Italian Pita Sticks, Caramel Nut Brownie Treats (page 84), Florentine Yogurt Dip and Italian Sausage Sandwiches (page 84).

ITALIAN SAUSAGE SANDWICHES

A hearty, satisfying sandwich.

1 pound Italian sausage, cut into
½-inch pieces
2 green bell peppers, cut into
julienne strips
1 onion, thinly sliced and separated
into rings
2 cans (8 ounces each) tomato sauce
¼ cup dry red wine

1 package (1.5 ounces) Lawry's
Spaghetti Sauce Seasoning
Blend with Imported
Mushrooms
8 French or sourdough rolls, cut in
half lengthwise
Grated Parmesan cheese

In large skillet, sauté sausage until browned, about 7 minutes. Add green peppers and onion; sauté 10 minutes longer. Drain fat. Add tomato sauce, wine and Spaghetti Sauce Seasoning Blend with Imported Mushrooms; blend well. Bring to a boil. Reduce heat; cover and simmer 20 minutes, stirring occasionally. Spoon sausage mixture over half of each roll. Sprinkle with Parmesan cheese and top with remaining half roll.   *Makes 8 servings*

PRESENTATION: For a buffet party, serve sausage, peppers and onion mixture in chafing dish. Serve sliced rolls and Parmesan cheese on the side.

CARAMEL NUT BROWNIE TREATS

A great lunch-box snack or party treat.

1 box (18.25 ounces) German
chocolate cake mix
½ cup butter or margarine, softened
½ teaspoon vanilla
⅔ cup evaporated milk

¾ cup chopped pecans or peanuts
1 package (14 ounces) caramel
candy squares, unwrapped
1 package (6 ounces) semi-sweet
chocolate chips

In medium bowl, combine cake mix, butter, vanilla and ⅓ cup of the evaporated milk; blend well. Stir in nuts. In 12×8×2-inch baking pan, spread ½ of batter. Bake, uncovered, in 350°F oven 6 minutes. Meanwhile, in top of double boiler over simmering water, combine caramels and remaining ⅓ cup evaporated milk. Heat until caramels are melted. Sprinkle chocolate chips over baked cake mixture; top with melted caramels. Spread remaining ½ of batter over caramel layer. Bake, uncovered, 10 to 15 minutes longer. Cool.
Makes 12 servings

PRESENTATION: Cut into 1-inch squares.

THURSDAY
Elegant Entertaining

CITRUS AND ONION SALAD

A refreshing and unusual salad combination.

½ cup vegetable oil
⅓ cup white wine vinegar
3 to 4 tablespoons sugar
1 teaspoon Lawry's Seasoned Salt
¾ teaspoon dry mustard
2 to 3 large navel oranges, peeled
  and thinly sliced crosswise

1 grapefruit, peeled and thinly
  sliced crosswise
1 medium red onion, thinly sliced
  and separated into rings
Spinach leaves

In small jar with tight-fitting lid, combine oil, vinegar, sugar, Seasoned Salt and mustard; shake to blend well. In shallow dish, layer oranges, grapefruit and onion; pour dressing over to coat. Cover and refrigerate 1 hour or overnight. Remove oranges, grapefruit and onion from marinade; reserve marinade. Arrange on individual salad plates lined with spinach leaves.

Makes 4 servings

PRESENTATION: Serve with reserved marinade on the side.

HINT: For extra flavor, try adding avocado slices or roasted cashews just before serving.

SLICED TOMATOES WITH A ZIP

A quicker-than-quick side dish.

3 tablespoons mayonnaise
2 tablespoons brown mustard
1 tablespoon chopped parsley
¾ teaspoon Lawry's Garlic Salt

½ teaspoon Lawry's Seasoned
  Pepper
2 large, firm tomatoes, sliced
  ¼ inch thick

In small bowl, combine all ingredients except tomatoes; blend well. Spread over tomato slices. Place slices on broiler pan and broil, 6 inches from heat, 3 minutes or until lightly browned. Serve immediately.

Makes 4 servings

PRESENTATION: Serve with chicken or meat dishes.

HINT: For extra flavor, sprinkle grated Parmesan cheese over tomatoes just before serving.

CHICKEN JERUSALEM

An elegant way to serve chicken.

3 tablespoons vegetable oil
2 pounds boneless chicken breasts, halved and skinned
½ cup dry white wine
1 can (4 ounces) sliced mushrooms, drained
1 can (8½ ounces) artichoke hearts, drained, or 1 package (9 ounces) frozen artichoke hearts, thawed

2 tablespoons all-purpose flour
½ teaspoon Lawry's Seasoned Salt
¼ teaspoon Lawry's Seasoned Pepper
½ cup milk
Paprika

In large skillet, heat oil and brown chicken lightly on both sides; drain. Add wine, mushrooms and artichokes. Bring to a boil. Reduce heat; cover and simmer 20 minutes. Remove chicken, mushrooms and artichokes to heated platter. Stir flour, Seasoned Salt and Seasoned Pepper into pan juices; heat 2 to 3 minutes, stirring constantly. Blend in milk; stir until thickened. On individual serving plates, arrange chicken, artichokes and mushrooms. Spoon sauce over chicken; sprinkle with paprika. *Makes 4 to 6 servings*

PRESENTATION: Serve with broiled tomatoes or hot cooked rice.

HINT: Dish may be frozen. It will keep, tightly covered, 6 to 8 weeks.

LEMON MOUSSE SOUFFLÉ

A simple and delicious dessert. Perfect after a late night dinner.

3 ounces Neufchâtel cheese, softened
1 cup lemon nonfat yogurt
2 tablespoons sifted powdered sugar

Juice of 1 lemon
8 ounces whipped dessert topping
1 to 2 teaspoons grated lemon peel
Fresh raspberries, strawberries or blueberries

In large bowl, combine Neufchâtel cheese, yogurt, sugar and lemon juice. Gently fold in whipped topping and lemon peel. Reserve some of the fruit for garnish; place remaining fruit in individual dessert glasses. Spoon mousse mixture on top of fruit. Refrigerate until ready to serve.

Makes 4 servings

PRESENTATION: Garnish with remaining fruit, lemon slices and mint sprigs.

On the dinner plates: Chicken Jerusalem and Sliced Tomatoes with a Zip (page 85). On the salad plates: Citrus and Onion Salad (page 85). In the dessert cups: Lemon Mousse Soufflé.

FRIDAY
Backyard Family Dinner

FLANK STEAK GRILL

For best flavor, marinate the flank steak overnight.

¼ cup red wine vinegar
¼ cup ketchup
1 tablespoon plus 1 teaspoon
  Worcestershire sauce
1 tablespoon plus 1 teaspoon liquid
  smoke seasoning (optional)

2 teaspoons Lawry's Garlic Powder
  with Parsley
1 teaspoon Lawry's Seasoned Salt
1 beef flank steak (about 2 pounds)

In 1-cup measure, combine vinegar, ketchup, Worcestershire sauce, liquid smoke, Garlic Powder with Parsley and Seasoned Salt; blend well. Place flank steak in plastic bag. Pour in marinade and seal bag tightly. Place bag in large bowl and refrigerate 30 minutes or overnight to marinate steak. Grill steak 8 to 10 minutes on each side for medium-rare, or to desired doneness, basting often with marinade. Cut steak diagonally into thin slices.

Makes 4 to 6 servings

PRESENTATION: Garnish with thyme sprigs and grilled fresh pineapple slices.

HINT: London broil or round steak can be substituted for the flank steak.

SHERBET SMOOTHIES

A refreshing ending to a summer meal.

2 pints lemon sherbet, softened
1½ cups cold milk

2 cups frozen fruit, such as peaches,
  blueberries or raspberries

In blender or food processor, combine all ingredients. Blend until smooth. Serve immediately in chilled glasses.

Makes 6 to 8 servings

PRESENTATION: Garnish with fresh mint. Serve a variety of sherbet smoothies with various toppings such as granola, chocolate chips, flaked coconut or cookie crumbs for a "make your own" sherbet cup.

Clockwise from top right: Sherbet Smoothies, Flank Steak Grill, Grilled Lemon Potatoes (page 90) and Summer Salad (page 90).

GRILLED LEMON POTATOES

A different and delicious way to serve potatoes.

3 large russet potatoes
⅓ cup butter or margarine
1 tablespoon lemon juice
1¼ teaspoons Lawry's Lemon Pepper
   Seasoning

½ teaspoon Lawry's Garlic Salt
½ teaspoon Lawry's Seasoned Salt

Cut potatoes in half lengthwise; deeply score cut surfaces. Cover skin side with aluminum foil. In small saucepan, melt butter; add remaining ingredients. Generously brush cut sides of potatoes with butter mixture. Grill potatoes until tender, about 45 minutes. Turn occasionally during grilling.

Makes 6 servings

PRESENTATION: Serve with any grilled meats, fish or poultry.

MICROWAVE DIRECTIONS: Microwave whole potatoes on HIGH 7 minutes. Cool slightly. Slice and brush as above; grill only 5 to 10 minutes or until heated through.

SUMMER SALAD

A wonderful salad with plenty of crunch.

3 cups broccoli flowerettes, cooked
   tender-crisp
1 large ripe tomato, diced
¼ cup coarsely grated Cheddar
   cheese
¼ cup diced red onion
⅔ cup vegetable oil
⅓ cup white wine vinegar

¼ cup grated Romano cheese
½ teaspoon Lawry's Seasoned Salt
¼ teaspoon Lawry's Garlic Powder
   with Parsley
¼ teaspoon dried oregano, crushed
1 box (6 ounces) seasoned croutons
   (optional)

In medium bowl, combine broccoli, tomato, Cheddar cheese and onion. In small bowl, combine oil, vinegar, Romano cheese, Seasoned Salt, Garlic Powder with Parsley and oregano; blend well. Pour over broccoli mixture; toss to coat. Cover and refrigerate until ready to serve. Add seasoned croutons just before serving.

Makes 6 servings

PRESENTATION: Serve with grilled meats, fish or poultry.

INDEX

We hope that you have enjoyed the Weekday Gourmet cookbooklet. We would appreciate any comments you have relating to the booklet or Lawry's Products. Please provide the following information so that we may better serve you.

Cookbooklet Comments: _____

Would you like to join our mailing list to receive product information, recipes, coupons and samples? ☐ Yes   ☐ No

What Lawry's products do you currently use? _____

NAME _____
Please print clearly

ADDRESS _____

CITY _____ STATE _____ ZIP _____

Call 1-800-9-LAWRYS with comments and questions, weekdays 8 A.M. to 5 P.M. P.S.T.